100 EASY RECIPES
chicken

bay books

contents

soups and starters 6

salads 28

pasta 42

stir-fries and pan-fries 56

grills and barbecues 76

one-pots 90

pies and roasts 110

index 126

soups and starters

herbed chicken soup

1 boneless, skinless chicken breast
1 bay leaf
6 black peppercorns
1 whole clove
4 parsley sprigs
2 tablespoons olive oil
1 onion, finely chopped
1 small carrot, finely chopped
1 celery stalk, finely chopped
1 large potato, finely chopped
1 teaspoon finely chopped rosemary,
  or ¼ teaspoon dried
1 teaspoon chopped thyme,
  or ½ teaspoon dried
1 teaspoon chopped marjoram,
  or ½ teaspoon dried
1 litre (35 fl oz/4 cups) chicken stock
310 g (11 oz) tinned creamed corn
4 tablespoons finely chopped flat-leaf
  (Italian) parsley

serves 6

method Trim the chicken breast of excess fat and sinew. Put 500 ml (17 fl oz/2 cups) water in a saucepan and bring to a simmer. Add the chicken, bay leaf, peppercorns, clove and parsley and cook for 8 minutes, or until the chicken is tender and cooked through. Remove the chicken from the liquid and cool slightly before shredding. Discard the bay leaf, peppercorns, clove and parsley, and reserve the cooking liquid.

Heat the oil in a large, heavy-based saucepan. Add the onion, carrot and celery and cook over medium heat for 5 minutes, or until the onion is soft. Add the potato, rosemary, thyme and marjoram and cook, stirring, over medium heat for 1 minute.

Add the stock and reserved cooking liquid. Season to taste with salt and pepper and bring to the boil. Reduce the heat and simmer for 15 minutes, or until the potato and carrot have softened. Add the corn and shredded chicken and stir for 2 minutes, or until heated through. Stir in the parsley.

hint *Use shredded barbecued chicken if you prefer, and add extra stock to make up the liquid.*

asian chicken and noodle soup

chilli paste

4 dried chillies, roughly chopped
1 teaspoon coriander seeds
1 teaspoon grated fresh ginger
1 spring onion (scallion), chopped
½ teaspoon ground turmeric

750 ml (26 fl oz/3 cups) coconut milk
350 g (12 oz) boneless, skinless chicken
breast, thinly sliced
2 tablespoons soy sauce
500 ml (17 fl oz/2 cups) chicken stock
400 g (14 oz) dried egg noodles
peanut oil, for deep-frying
spring onion (scallion), to serve
red chillies, to serve

serves 4

method To make the chilli paste, put all the ingredients in a small saucepan. Stir over low heat for 5 minutes, or until fragrant. Transfer to a mortar and pestle or food processor and grind until smooth.

Heat 250 ml (9 fl oz/1 cup) of the coconut milk in a saucepan. Add the prepared chilli paste and stir for 2–3 minutes. Add the sliced chicken and soy sauce and cook for 3–4 minutes. Stir in the remaining coconut milk and the stock. Bring to the boil, reduce the heat and simmer for 10 minutes.

Break a quarter of the noodles into large pieces and fry in the hot peanut oil until crisp, then drain on paper towels. Cook the remaining noodles in boiling water until just tender, then drain.

Place the boiled noodles in serving bowls and ladle the hot soup over the top. Garnish with the fried noodles and serve with spring onion and chilli.

roasted capsicum and smoked chicken soup

4 large red capsicums (peppers)
1 long green chilli
1 tablespoon olive oil
1 large onion, roughly chopped
2 garlic cloves, crushed
½ teaspoon cayenne pepper
1 teaspoon ground coriander
1 teaspoon ground cumin
2 litres (8 cups) chicken stock
315 g (11 oz) smoked chicken, cubed
1 handful coriander (cilantro) leaves
sour cream and tortilla chips, to serve

serves 6–8

method Remove the seeds and membrane from the capsicums and the chilli, and cut into large flattish pieces. Cook, skin-side-up, under a hot grill (broiler) until the skin blackens and blisters. Remove from the heat, place in a plastic bag and leave to cool, then peel away the skin. Roughly chop the capsicum, and finely slice the chilli.

Heat the olive oil in a large saucepan over medium heat. Fry the onion and garlic for 2–3 minutes. Mix in the cayenne pepper, coriander and cumin and cook for a further 1 minute, stirring constantly. Add the stock, capsicum and chilli and bring to the boil. Reduce the heat and simmer for 15 minutes.

Remove from the heat, leave to cool slightly, then purée in a blender or food processor in batches until it becomes a smooth soup. Return the soup to the pan.

Reheat the soup over medium heat for 10 minutes. Stir in the chicken and season with pepper. When the soup is hot and ready to serve, add the coriander leaves. Ladle the soup into serving bowls and top each with sour cream. Serve with the tortilla chips.

thai chicken and coconut soup

5 cm (2 inch) piece galangal (see Hint)
500 ml (17 fl oz/2 cups) coconut milk
250 ml (9 fl oz/1 cup) chicken stock
3 boneless, skinless chicken breasts,
cut into thin strips
1–2 teaspoons finely chopped red chilli
2 tablespoons fish sauce
1 teaspoon soft brown sugar
1 small handful coriander (cilantro) leaves

serves 4

method Peel the galangal and cut it into thin slices. Combine the galangal, coconut milk and chicken stock in a medium saucepan. Bring to the boil and simmer, uncovered, over low heat for 10 minutes, stirring occasionally.

Add the chicken strips and chilli to the pan and simmer for 8 minutes.

Stir in the fish sauce and brown sugar. Add the coriander leaves and serve immediately.

hint *If fresh galangal is not available, you can use 5 large slices of dried galangal instead. Prepare by soaking the slices in a little boiling water for 10 minutes and then cutting them into shreds. Add the soaking liquid to the chicken stock to make 250 ml (9 fl oz/1 cup) and use it in the recipe.*

mulligatawny

1 kg (2 lb 4 oz) chicken pieces
2 tablespoons plain (all-purpose) flour
2 teaspoons curry powder
½ teaspoon ground ginger
1 teaspoon ground turmeric
60 g (2 oz) butter
12 black peppercorns
6 whole cloves
1.5 litres (6 cups) chicken stock
1 large apple, peeled, cored and chopped
2 tablespoons lemon juice
125 ml (4 fl oz/½ cup) cream
steamed rice, to serve

serves 6

method Trim the chicken pieces of any excess fat and sinew. In a bowl, combine the flour, curry powder, ginger and turmeric, and rub the mix into the chicken.

Heat the butter in a large saucepan and cook the chicken until lightly browned on all sides. Tie the peppercorns and cloves together in a small piece of muslin and add to the pan with the stock. Bring to the boil, then reduce the heat slightly and simmer, covered, for 1 hour. Add the apple and cook for a further 15 minutes.

Remove the chicken from the pan and discard the muslin bag. When the chicken is cool enough to handle, remove the skin and bones from the chicken and finely shred the flesh. Skim any fat from the surface of the soup.

Return the chicken to the pan. Stir in the lemon juice and cream, and heat through gently, without boiling. Serve with rice.

spicy chicken broth with coriander pasta

350 g (12 oz) boneless, skinless
chicken thighs or wings
2 carrots, finely chopped
2 celery stalks, finely chopped
2 small leeks, finely chopped
3 egg whites
1.5 litres (6 cups) chicken stock
Tabasco sauce

coriander pasta

60 g (2 oz/½ cup) plain (all-purpose) flour
1 egg
½ teaspoon sesame oil
1 large handful coriander (cilantro) leaves

serves 4

method Put the chicken, carrot, celery and leek in a large saucepan. Push the chicken to one side and add the egg whites to the vegetables. Using a wire whisk, beat until frothy (take care not to use a pan that can be scratched by the whisk).

Warm the chicken stock in another saucepan, then add gradually to the first pan, whisking constantly to froth the egg whites. Continue whisking while slowly bringing to the boil. Make a hole in the top of the froth with a spoon and then leave to simmer, uncovered, for 30 minutes without stirring. Line a strainer with a damp tea towel (dish towel) and strain the broth into a bowl. Discard the chicken and vegetables. Season to taste with salt, pepper and Tabasco. Set aside.

To make the coriander pasta, sift the flour into a bowl and make a well in the centre. Whisk the egg and sesame oil together and pour into the well. Mix to a soft dough and knead on a floured surface for 2 minutes, or until smooth.

Divide the pasta dough into four even portions. Roll one portion out very thinly (use a pasta machine if you have one) and cover with a layer of evenly spaced coriander leaves. Roll out another portion of pasta and lay this on top of the leaves. Repeat with the remaining pasta and coriander.

Cut squares of pasta around the coriander leaves. Bring the chicken broth gently to a simmer. Add the pasta, cook for 1 minute and serve.

chicken curry laksa

2 boneless, skinless chicken breasts
1 large onion, roughly chopped
5 cm (2 inch) piece ginger, chopped
8 cm (3 inch) piece galangal, peeled
   and chopped
1 lemongrass stem, white part only,
   roughly chopped
2 garlic cloves
1 red chilli, seeded and chopped
2 teaspoons oil
2 tablespoons mild curry paste
500 ml (17 fl oz/2 cups) chicken stock
60 g (2 oz) rice vermicelli
50 g (2 oz) dried egg noodles
400 ml (14 fl oz) light coconut milk
10 snow peas (mangetouts), halved
3 spring onions (scallions), finely chopped
90 g (3 oz/1 cup) bean sprouts
1 small handful coriander (cilantro) leaves

serves 4

method Cut the chicken into bite-sized cubes. Process the onion, ginger, galangal, lemongrass, garlic and chilli in a food processor until finely chopped. Add the oil and process until the mixture is a paste-like consistency. Spoon into a large wok, add the curry paste and stir over low heat for 1–2 minutes, or until aromatic. Take care not to burn the mixture.

Increase the heat to medium, add the chicken and stir for 2 minutes, until the chicken is well coated. Stir in the chicken stock and mix well. Bring slowly to the boil, then simmer for 10 minutes, or until the chicken is cooked through.

Meanwhile, cut the vermicelli into shorter lengths using scissors. Cook the vermicelli and the egg noodles separately in large saucepans of boiling water for 5 minutes each. Drain and rinse under cold water.

Just prior to serving, add the coconut milk and snow peas to the chicken mixture and heat through. To serve, divide the vermicelli and egg noodles among four warmed serving bowls. Pour the hot laksa over the top and garnish with the spring onion, bean sprouts and coriander leaves.

hint If you prefer a more fiery laksa, use a medium or hot brand of curry paste or increase the amount of chilli. Stir the curry paste into the onion mixture, over low heat, until aromatic.

100 EASY RECIPES CHICKEN

chicken noodle soup

1.25 kg (2 lb 12 oz) chicken wings
2 celery stalks, chopped
1 carrot, chopped
1 onion, chopped
1 bay leaf
1 thyme sprig
4 parsley sprigs
45 g (1½ oz) dried fine egg noodles
1 boneless, skinless chicken breast,
finely chopped
snipped chives, to serve

serves 4–6

method Rinse the chicken wings and place in a large saucepan with the celery, carrot, onion, bay leaf, thyme, parsley, 1 teaspoon salt and 2 litres (8 cups) of water. Bring to the boil slowly, skimming the surface as required. Simmer, covered, for 1 hour. Allow to cool slightly, then strain and discard the chicken and the vegetables.

Cool the stock further, then cover and refrigerate for at least 1 hour, or until fat forms on the surface of the chilled stock that can be skimmed off with a spoon.

Place the stock in a large saucepan and bring to the boil. Gently crush the noodles and add to the soup. Return to the boil and simmer for 8 minutes, or until tender. Add the chopped chicken and simmer for a further 4–5 minutes, or until the chicken is cooked through. Serve topped with the chives.

creamy spinach and chicken soup

1 tablespoon oil
1 kg (2 lb/4 oz) chicken pieces
1 carrot, chopped
2 celery stalks, chopped
1 onion, chopped
6 black peppercorns
2 garlic cloves, chopped
bouquet garni
800 g (1 lb 12 oz) sweet potato, chopped
500 g (1 lb 2 oz) English spinach
125 ml (4 fl oz/½ cup) cream

serves 6

method   Heat the oil in a large saucepan, add the chicken pieces in batches and brown well. Drain on paper towels. Pour off the excess fat, leaving 1 tablespoon in the pan. Return the chicken to the pan with the carrot, celery, onion, peppercorns, garlic, bouquet garni and 1.5 litres (6 cups) of water.

Bring the soup to the boil, reduce the heat and simmer for 40 minutes. Strain, discarding the vegetables, peppercorns and bouquet garni. Return the stock to the pan. Pull the chicken meat from the bones, shred and set aside.

Add the sweet potato to the stock in the pan. Bring to the boil, then reduce the heat and simmer until tender. Add the spinach leaves and cook until wilted. Process the spinach in batches in a food processor until finely chopped.

Return the spinach to the pan, add the shredded chicken and stir in the cream. Season to taste. Reheat gently before serving but do not allow the soup to boil.

chicken and vegetable soup

1.5 kg (3 lb 5 oz) chicken
2 carrots, roughly chopped
2 celery stalks, roughly chopped
1 onion, quartered
1 parsley sprig
2 bay leaves
4 black peppercorns
50 g (2 oz) butter
2 tablespoons plain (all-purpose) flour
2 potatoes, chopped
250 g (9 oz) butternut pumpkin (squash),
cut into bite-sized pieces
2 carrots, extra, cut into thin matchsticks
1 leek, cut into small lengths
3 celery stalks, extra, cut into thin
matchsticks
100 g (4 oz) green beans, cut into short
lengths, or baby green beans, halved
200 g (7 oz) broccoli, cut into small florets
100 g (4 oz) sugar snap peas, trimmed
50 g (2 oz) English spinach leaves, shredded
125 ml (4 fl oz/½ cup) cream
4 tablespoons chopped flat-leaf
(Italian) parsley

serves 6–8

method   Place the chicken in a large saucepan with the carrot, celery, onion, parsley, bay leaves, 2 teaspoons of salt and the peppercorns. Add 3 litres (12 cups) of water. Bring to the boil, then reduce the heat and simmer for 1 hour, skimming the surface as required. Allow to cool for at least 30 minutes. Strain through a sieve and reserve the liquid for stock, discard the vegetables.

Remove the chicken and allow to cool until it is cool enough to handle. Discard the skin, then cut or pull the flesh from the bones and shred into small pieces. Cover and set the chicken meat aside.

Heat the butter in a large saucepan over medium heat and, when foaming, add the flour. Cook, stirring, for 1 minute. Remove from the heat and gradually stir in the stock you made earlier. Return to the heat and bring to the boil, stirring constantly. Add the potato, pumpkin and the extra carrot and simmer for 7 minutes. Add the leek, extra celery and beans and simmer for 5 minutes. Finally, add the broccoli and sugar snap peas and cook for a further 3 minutes.

Just before serving, add the chicken, spinach, cream and chopped parsley. Reheat the soup gently but do not allow it to boil. Keep stirring until the spinach has wilted. Season to taste with salt and black pepper. Serve the soup immediately and sprinkle with chopped parsley.

chicken and lemon meatballs

500 g (1 lb 2 oz) minced (ground) chicken
2 garlic cloves, crushed
80 g (3 oz/1 cup) fresh white breadcrumbs
1 teaspoon grated lemon zest
1 teaspoon lemon thyme
1 egg, lightly beaten
1 tablespoon olive oil
2 tablespoons lemon juice

yoghurt mint sauce

200 g (7 oz) plain yoghurt
1 tablespoon shredded mint
rinsed, chopped zest from ¼ of a
    preserved lemon

serves 4

method Using your hands, mix the minced chicken, garlic, breadcrumbs, lemon zest, thyme, egg and some salt and freshly ground pepper together in a large bowl. Wet your hands and form tablespoons of the mixture into balls and place on a lined tray. Refrigerate for 30 minutes.

To make the yoghurt mint sauce, mix the yoghurt, mint and preserved lemon zest together.

Heat the oil in a non-stick frying pan and cook the chicken meatballs in two batches until golden on all sides and cooked through. Sprinkle the meatballs with the lemon juice, transfer them to a serving dish and sprinkle with more salt. Serve with the yoghurt mint sauce.

chicken curry bags

125 g (5 oz/1 cup) plain (all-purpose) flour
1 egg
1 egg yolk
310 ml (11 fl oz/1¼ cups) milk
50 g (2 oz) butter, melted
butter, extra, for greasing

chicken filling

60 g (2 oz) butter
1 red onion, chopped
1–2 teaspoons curry powder
2 tablespoons plain (all-purpose) flour
310 ml (11 fl oz/1¼ cups) milk
60 ml (2 fl oz/¼ cup) cream
1 large cooked boneless, skinless chicken
breast, finely cubed
1 small handful chopped parsley
2 hard-boiled eggs, chopped

makes 10

method   Whisk together the flour, egg, egg yolk and half the milk in a bowl. Add the remaining milk and 1 tablespoon melted butter and whisk until smooth. Cover and set aside for 30 minutes.

To make the chicken filling, melt the butter in a frying pan over medium heat, add the onion and cook until soft. Add the curry powder and flour and cook for 1 minute. Gradually add the milk, stirring, until smooth. Cook until the sauce has boiled and thickened. Remove from the heat, add the cream, chicken, parsley and egg.

Heat a crepe pan and brush with butter. Pour 60 ml (2 fl oz/¼ cup) batter into the pan, swirling the pan to cover the base. Pour the excess batter back into the jug, adding a little more milk if too thick. Cook for about 30 seconds, then turn over and cook the other side until lightly brown.

Preheat the oven to 180°C (350°F/Gas 4). Place 3 tablespoons of the chicken filling in the centre of each crepe, gather up into a bag and tie with kitchen string. Grease a baking dish, brush each bag with butter and bake for 10 minutes, or until cooked through.

chicken satay with peanut sauce

500 g (1 lb 2 oz) boneless, skinless chicken
   thighs, trimmed
1 onion, roughly chopped
2 lemongrass stems, white part only,
   thinly sliced
4 garlic cloves
2 red chillies, chopped
2 teaspoons ground coriander
1 teaspoon ground cumin
1 tablespoon soy sauce
60 ml (2 fl oz/¼ cup) oil
1 tablespoon soft brown sugar
Lebanese (short) cucumber slices, to serve
chopped roasted peanuts, to serve

peanut sauce

125 g (5 oz/½ cup) crunchy peanut butter
250 ml (9 fl oz/1 cup) coconut milk
1–2 tablespoons sweet chilli sauce
1 tablespoon soy sauce
2 teaspoons lemon juice

serves 4

method Soak 20 wooden skewers in water for 20 minutes to prevent scorching. Cut the chicken into thick flattish strips. Thread a strip of chicken onto each skewer, flattening it on the skewer.

Process the onion, lemongrass, garlic, chilli, coriander, cumin, salt and soy sauce in a food processor, in short bursts, until smooth, adding a little oil to assist the processing. Spread the lemongrass mixture over the chicken, cover and refrigerate for 30 minutes.

To make the peanut sauce, put the peanut butter, coconut milk, chilli sauce, soy sauce and lemon juice in a heavy-based saucepan with 125 ml (4 fl oz/½ cup) water. Stir over low heat until the mixture boils. Remove from the heat. The sauce will thicken on standing.

Heat a chargrill plate or barbecue flatplate until very hot and brush with the remaining oil. Cook the chicken in batches for 2–3 minutes on each side, sprinkling with a little oil and brown sugar (this will help produce a lovely flavour and colour). Serve garnished with the cucumber and peanuts. Serve the peanut sauce as a dipping sauce.

chicken liver pâté with pistachio nuts

6 very thin slices prosciutto
40 g (1 oz) butter
60 ml (2 fl oz/¼ cup) olive oil
80 g (3 oz) finely diced bacon
1 onion, finely chopped
2 garlic cloves, crushed
500 g (1 lb 2 oz) chicken livers
3 bay leaves
80 ml (3 fl oz/⅓ cup) sherry or brandy
125 g (5 oz) butter, extra, softened
50 g (2 oz/⅓ cup) pistachio nuts, toasted

serves 10

method   Line a 1.5 litre (6 cup) loaf tin with foil. Then line with the prosciutto so that it hangs over the sides, making sure each slice overlaps. Heat the butter and olive oil in a heavy-based saucepan and cook the bacon, onion and garlic for 5–6 minutes, or until the onion is softened but not browned.

Trim the chicken livers of any fat and veins. Add them to the saucepan with the bay leaves. Increase the heat to hot and cook the liver for 3–4 minutes, or until the livers are brown on the outside, but still pink on the inside. Add the sherry and simmer, stirring, for about 3 minutes, or until the liquid has almost evaporated. Remove the bay leaves.

Process the chicken mixture in a food processor until very fine. Gradually add the extra butter and then blend until smooth. Season, then stir in the pistachio nuts.

Spoon the pâté into the tin and fold the prosciutto over to enclose it. Refrigerate for at least 3–4 hours before serving. Cut into slices to serve.

note   *The flavour, colour and texture of the pâté will improve after two days, and will also become easier to slice. Keep refrigerated for three to four days.*

chicken quesadillas

4 large green chillies
3 large red chillies
2 boneless, skinless chicken breasts
60 g (2 oz/¼ cup) wholegrain mustard
2 tablespoons honey
6 spring onions (scallions), thinly sliced
1–2 small red chillies, thinly sliced, optional
1–2 small green chillies, thinly sliced, optional
375 g (13 oz/3 cups) grated cheddar cheese
4 flour tortillas
olive oil, for cooking

green chilli salsa

3 long green chillies, thinly sliced
2 tomatoes, peeled, seeded and chopped
1 onion, finely chopped
4 tablespoons coriander (cilantro) leaves,
   finely chopped
2 tablespoons lime juice

serves 4

method   Put the large chillies under a hot grill (broiler). Cook for 5–8 minutes, turning frequently, until the skins are blackened, then allow to cool in a plastic bag. Remove the skin and seeds. Cut the chillies in half, then slice into thin strips. Place the chicken in a shallow non-metallic dish. Combine the mustard and honey and add to the chicken. Turn the meat until it is well coated with the mixture. Cover and refrigerate for 1 hour. Place the chicken under a hot grill and cook for 4 minutes each side, or until cooked through and tender. Cool, then cut into thin strips.

To make the green chilli salsa, combine the ingredients in a bowl and mix well, adding a little more lime juice if desired. Set aside.

Mix the chicken, spring onion, roasted chilli, sliced chilli and the cheddar together in a large bowl. Lightly grease a large, heavy-based frying pan and warm over medium heat. Place one tortilla in the pan and sprinkle with half of the chicken mix and top with another tortilla. Brush lightly with a little oil, invert the quesadilla onto a plate and then slide back into the pan so that the top becomes the bottom. Cook for a few minutes longer, just until the cheddar has melted and the underside looks golden and crisp. Slide the quesadilla onto a plate and keep warm.

Repeat with another tortilla and the remaining chicken mix. Top with the last tortilla. Cut into quarters and serve immediately, with the salsa.

pumpkin and pesto chicken in filo pastry

4 boneless, skinless chicken breasts
1 tablespoon oil
250 g (9 oz) pumpkin (winter squash)
500 g (1 lb 2 oz) English spinach
12 sheets filo pastry
100 g (4 oz) butter, melted
25 g (1 oz/¼ cup) dry breadcrumbs
100 g (4 oz) ricotta cheese
90 g (3 oz/⅓ cup) good-quality pesto
1 tablespoon pine nuts, chopped

serves 4

method Preheat the oven to 200°C (400°F/Gas 6). Season the chicken breast with salt and freshly ground pepper. Heat half the oil in a non-stick frying pan and fry the chicken until browned on both sides, then remove from the pan.

Cut the peeled pumpkin into 5 mm (¼ inch) slices. Heat the remaining oil in the same pan and fry the pumpkin until lightly browned on both sides. Allow to cool.

Put the spinach leaves in a bowl of boiling water and stir until just wilted. Drain well and pat dry with paper towels. Layer 3 sheets of filo pastry, brushing each with some of the melted butter, sprinkling between layers with some of the breadcrumbs.

Wrap each chicken breast in a quarter of the spinach and place one on a short side of the filo, leaving a 2 cm (¾ inch) gap. Top the chicken with a quarter of the pumpkin slices, then spread a quarter of the ricotta down the centre of the pumpkin. Top with a tablespoon of the pesto.

Fold the sides of the pastry over the filling, then roll up the parcel until it sits on the unsecured end. Repeat with the remaining ingredients. Place the parcels on a lightly greased baking tray, brush with any remaining butter and sprinkle with the pine nuts. Bake for 15 minutes, cover loosely with foil and bake for a further 20 minutes, or until the pastry is golden brown.

lemongrass chicken skewers

4 boneless, skinless chicken thighs
  (400 g/14 oz)
1½ tablespoons soft brown sugar
1½ tablespoons lime juice
2 teaspoons green curry paste
18 makrut (kaffir lime) leaves
2 stems lemongrass

mango salsa

1 small mango, finely diced
1 teaspoon grated lime zest
2 teaspoons lime juice
1 teaspoon soft brown sugar
½ teaspoon fish sauce

serves 4

method   Discard any excess fat from the chicken and cut in half lengthways. Combine the sugar, lime juice, curry paste and 2 of the finely shredded makrut leaves, in a bowl. Add the chicken and mix well. Cover and refrigerate for several hours or overnight.

To make the mango salsa, put all the ingredients in a bowl and stir gently to combine.

Trim the lemongrass to 20 cm (8 inches), leaving the root end intact. Cut each stem lengthways into four pieces. Cut a slit in each of the remaining lime leaves and thread one onto each piece of lemon grass. Cut two slits in each piece of chicken and thread onto the lemongrass, followed by another makrut leaf.

Preheat a barbecue flat plate or a large frying pan on medium–high. Cook the chicken skewers, turning occasionally, for 10 minutes or until the chicken is golden and cooked through. Serve the skewers with the mango salsa.

chicken and leek parcels

1 tablespoon oil, plus extra, for greasing
3 boneless, skinless chicken thighs
(330 g/12 oz)
30 g (1 oz) butter
2 leeks, thinly sliced
1 bacon slice, finely chopped
1 garlic clove, crushed
60 ml (2 fl oz/¼ cup) white wine
60 ml (2 fl oz/¼ cup) cream
2 teaspoons wholegrain mustard
25 g (1 oz/¼ cup) grated parmesan cheese
10 sheets filo pastry
80 g (3 oz) butter, extra, melted

makes 20

method Preheat oven to 180°C (350°F/Gas 4). Brush a baking tray with oil. Heat the oil in a heavy-based frying pan. Cook the chicken for 5 minutes on each side, or until browned and tender. Remove from the pan and drain on paper towels. Allow to cool, then chop the chicken finely.

Heat the butter in a large heavy-based saucepan. Add the leek, bacon and crushed garlic, and cook for 3–4 minutes, or until the leek is soft and the bacon is crisp. Add the chicken, wine, cream and mustard. Cook, stirring constantly, for 4 minutes, or until thickened. Remove from the heat. Season to taste with salt and freshly ground pepper, and stir in the parmesan. Set aside to cool slightly.

Lay a sheet of filo pastry on a work surface and brush with melted butter. Top with another sheet of pastry and brush with butter. Cut the pastry lengthways into 4 strips. Place 1 tablespoon of the chicken mixture at the end of each strip. Fold the end diagonally over the filling, then continue folding to the end of the strip, forming a triangle. Repeat with the remaining pastry and filling. Place the triangles on a greased baking tray and brush with butter. Bake the parcels in batches for 25 minutes, or until they are browned and heated through.

chicken curry puffs

2 tablespoons oil
400 g (14 oz) minced (ground) chicken
2 garlic cloves, crushed
1 onion, finely chopped
3 coriander (cilantro) roots, finely chopped
2 teaspoons ground turmeric
1½ teaspoons ground cumin
3 teaspoons ground coriander
1 small potato, peeled and very finely diced
1 tablespoon chopped coriander (cilantro)
    leaves and stems
3 teaspoons soft brown sugar
2 small red chillies, finely chopped
60 ml (2 fl oz/¼ cup) fish sauce
1 tablespoon lime juice
oil, extra, for deep-frying
chilli sauce or satay sauce, to serve

pastry

185 g (7 oz/1½ cups) plain (all-purpose)
    flour
90 g (3 oz/½ cup) rice flour
½ teaspoon salt
60 g (2 oz) butter
125 ml (4 fl oz/½ cup) coconut milk

makes 36

method   Heat the oil in a wok or pan. Add the chicken and cook over high heat for 3 minutes, breaking up any lumps. Add the garlic, onion, coriander roots, turmeric, cumin, coriander and the potato to the wok. Stir-fry over medium heat for 5 minutes, until the chicken and potato are cooked through.

Add the fresh coriander, sugar, black pepper, chilli, fish sauce and lime juice. Stir until well combined and most of the liquid has evaporated, remove from the heat and let cool.

To make the pastry, sift the flours, salt and pepper into a bowl and rub in the butter until the mixture is fine and crumbly. Make a well in the centre, add the coconut milk and mix with a knife until the mixture forms a dough. Cover with plastic wrap and refrigerate for 30 minutes.

Divide the dough in half. Roll one half on a lightly floured work surface to 3 mm (⅛ inch) thick, then cut into circles with an 8 cm (3 inch) cutter. Place 2 teaspoons of the filling in the centre of each circle, brush the edges of the pastry lightly with water and fold over to enclose the filling, pressing the edges to seal. Repeat with the remaining dough and filling, re-rolling the dough scraps.

Heat the oil in a large wok or pan (it should be only half full). Deep-fry the puffs, in batches, until they are puffed and browned. Remove from the oil with a wire mesh drainer; drain on paper towels. Serve with chilli or satay sauce.

chicken tikka

¼ onion, chopped
2 garlic cloves, crushed
1 tablespoon grated fresh ginger
2 tablespoons lemon juice
1 teaspoon grated lemon zest
3 teaspoons ground coriander
3 teaspoons ground cumin
3 teaspoons garam masala
90 g (3 oz/⅓ cup) plain yoghurt
750 g (1 lb 10 oz) boneless, skinless chicken
thighs, cut into cubes

makes 10

method   Soak 10 wooden skewers in cold water for 20 minutes to prevent scorching.

In a food processor, finely chop the onion, garlic, ginger, lemon juice, zest, coriander, cumin and garam masala. Stir in the yoghurt and 1 teaspoon of salt.

Thread 4–5 chicken cubes onto each skewer and place in a large shallow non-metallic dish. Coat the skewers with the spice mixture. Marinate for several hours or overnight, covered, in the refrigerator.

Cook the skewers in batches on a medium-hot barbecue flat plate or chargrill pan, or under a hot grill (broiler), for 3–4 minutes on each side, or until golden brown and cooked through.

salads

chicken and snow pea salad

150 g (5 oz) snow peas (mangetouts),
    trimmed
1 tablespoon oil
20 g (1 oz) butter
4 boneless, skinless chicken breasts
1 carrot, cut into thin matchsticks
2 celery stalks, cut into thin matchsticks
3 spring onions (scallions), cut into thin
    matchsticks
150 g (5 oz) button mushrooms, sliced
2 tablespoons flat-leaf (Italian) parsley,
    chopped
1 tablespoon chopped tarragon
150 g (5 oz) watercress or baby English
    spinach leaves, picked over
2 tablespoons almonds, chopped

dressing

60 ml (2 fl oz/¼ cup) extra virgin olive oil
1 tablespoon white wine vinegar
½ teaspoon sugar
60 g (2 oz/¼ cup) mayonnaise
2 tablespoons sour cream
1 tablespoon mustard

serves 6

method Blanch the snow peas until tender but still crisp. Rinse under cold water and drain well. Cut into strips.

Heat the oil and butter in a frying pan, add the chicken and cook for 7 minutes on each side, or until cooked through and well browned. Drain on paper towels. Cut into thin slices. Mix together the carrot, snow peas, chicken, celery, spring onion, mushrooms, parsley and tarragon, and season to taste with salt and pepper.

To make the dressing, combine the oil, vinegar and sugar. Stir well, then season. Add the mayonnaise, sour cream and mustard and stir until well blended. Plate the watercress, top with the chicken salad and drizzle with the dressing and chopped almonds.

100 EASY RECIPES CHICKEN

chicken and citrus salad with curry dressing

4 boneless, skinless chicken breasts
1 tablespoon olive oil
2 oranges
1 lettuce
250 g (9 oz) watercress, picked over
1 handful chives

curry dressing

3 teaspoons curry powder
2 spring onions (scallions), thinly sliced
2 tablespoons olive oil
2 tablespoons sunflower oil
1 tablespoon balsamic vinegar
2 teaspoons soft brown sugar
1 teaspoon chopped green chilli

serves 4

method Trim the chicken breasts of any fat and sinew. Heat the oil in a frying pan and cook the chicken over medium heat for about 7 minutes on each side, or until browned and tender. Allow to cool, then cut across the grain into thick strips.

To make the dressing, dry-fry the curry powder in a frying pan for 1 minute, or until fragrant. Cool slightly, then place in a small bowl with the remaining ingredients and whisk to combine. Season to taste with salt and pepper. Set aside to allow the flavours to develop.

Peel the oranges, removing all the white pith. Cut into segments, between the membrane, and discard any pips.

Wash and dry the lettuce and watercress and arrange on a large platter. Place the chicken pieces and orange segments on top. Whisk the dressing again, then drizzle it over the salad. Cut the chives into short lengths and scatter over the top.

tandoori chicken salad

4 boneless, skinless chicken breasts
2–3 tablespoons tandoori paste
200 g (7 oz) thick plain yoghurt
1 tablespoon lemon juice
1 handful coriander (cilantro) leaves
60 g (2 oz/½ cup) slivered almonds, toasted
snow pea (mangetout) sprouts, to serve

cucumber and yoghurt dressing

1 Lebanese (short) cucumber, grated
200 g (7 oz) thick plain yoghurt
1 tablespoon chopped mint
2 teaspoons lemon juice

serves 4

method   Cut the chicken breast into thick strips. Combine the tandoori paste, yoghurt and lemon juice in a large non-metallic bowl, add the chicken strips and toss to coat well. Refrigerate, covered, and leave to marinate overnight.

To make the dressing, put the grated cucumber in a medium bowl. Add the remaining ingredients and stir until well combined. Refrigerate until needed.

Heat a large non-stick frying pan, add the marinated chicken in batches and cook, turning, until cooked through. Cool and place in a large bowl. Add the coriander leaves and toasted almonds, and toss until combined. Serve on a bed of snow pea sprouts, with a dollop of dressing on top or served separately.

note   *The quality of the tandoori paste used will determine the flavour and look of the chicken. There are many home-made varieties available from supermarkets and delicatessens.*

succulent chicken and pasta salad

1 boneless, skinless chicken breast
375 ml (13 fl oz/1½ cups) chicken stock
350 g (12 oz) fusilli pasta
150 g (5 oz) asparagus, cut into short lengths
150 g (5 oz/heaped 1 cup) grated
gruyère cheese
2 spring onions (scallions), thinly sliced

dressing

60 ml (2 fl oz/¼ cup) olive oil
60 ml (2 fl oz/¼ cup) lemon juice
½ teaspoon sugar

serves 4

method Put the chicken and stock in a frying pan. Bring to the boil, then reduce the heat and poach gently, turning regularly, for 8 minutes, until tender and cooked through. Remove the chicken, cool and slice thinly.

Cook the pasta in a large saucepan of boiling salted water for 10–12 minutes, or until al dente. Drain and cool.

Cook the asparagus in boiling water for 2 minutes. Drain and place in a bowl of iced water. Drain again. Combine with the chicken, pasta, cheese and spring onions in a large bowl.

To make the dressing, whisk the ingredients together. Season to taste with salt and pepper. Add to the salad and toss well. Transfer to a serving bowl and serve.

smoked chicken caesar salad

garlic croutons

1 thin baguette
45 g (1 ½ oz) unsalted butter
125 ml (4 fl oz/½ cup) olive oil
4 garlic cloves, crushed

1 cos (romaine) lettuce, tough outer
  leaves discarded
1 large smoked chicken (about 950 g/
  2 lb 2 oz), cut into bite-sized pieces
150 g (5 oz) parmesan cheese, shaved

dressing

2 eggs
2 garlic cloves, crushed
2 tablespoons lemon juice
2 teaspoons dijon mustard
45 g (1 ½ oz) tinned anchovy fillets, drained
250 ml (9 fl oz/1 cup) olive oil

serves 4

method To make the garlic croutons, slice the baguette diagonally into 1 cm (½ inch) thick slices. Melt the butter and olive oil in a large frying pan over moderate heat. Stir in the garlic. Fry the bread, in batches, until golden. Remove from the pan and drain on paper towels.

Separate the lettuce leaves, wash and dry thoroughly. Tear the larger leaves into pieces and refrigerate until well chilled.

To make the dressing, process the eggs, garlic, lemon juice, mustard and anchovies. With the motor running, gradually pour in the oil in a thin stream and process until thick. Season to taste.

Combine the lettuce, chicken, half of the croutons and half the parmesan in a bowl and toss with the dressing. Spoon the salad in serving bowls and sprinkle with the remaining croutons and parmesan.

thai chicken salad

1 cos (romaine) lettuce
2 tablespoons oil
1.3 kg (3 lb) minced (ground) chicken
1 small handfull coriander (cilantro) leaves,
finely chopped
1 small handful mint, finely chopped
1 small red onion, sliced
3 spring onions (scallions), chopped
80 ml (3 fl oz/⅓ cup) lime juice
2 tablespoons soy sauce
2 tablespoons fish sauce
1 tablespoon sweet chilli sauce
2 garlic cloves, crushed
2 teaspoons soft brown sugar
1 tablespoon finely chopped lemongrass,
white part only
40 g (1½ oz/¼ cup) roasted peanuts

serves 6

method Wash and dry the lettuce leaves thoroughly. Arrange on a platter.

Heat the oil in a heavy-based frying pan. Add the minced chicken and 80 ml (3 fl oz/⅓ cup) water. Cook over medium heat for 5 minutes, or until the chicken is cooked and almost all the liquid has evaporated. Break up any lumps as the chicken cooks. Remove from the heat.

Transfer the chicken to a bowl. Stir in the coriander, mint, onion and spring onion.

Combine the lime juice, soy sauce, fish sauce, sweet chilli sauce, garlic, brown sugar and lemongrass in a small bowl. Season with salt and mix well. Stir into the chicken mixture. Just before serving, stir in the peanuts. Serve on the lettuce leaves.

vietnamese papaya and chicken salad

2 boneless, skinless chicken breasts
1 large green papaya
1 large handful Vietnamese mint
1 handful coriander (cilantro) leaves
2 red chillies, seeded and thinly sliced
2 tablespoons chopped roasted peanuts

dressing

2 tablespoons fish sauce
1 tablespoon rice wine vinegar
1 tablespoon lime juice
2 teaspoons sugar

serves 4

method Place the chicken in a frying pan with enough water to just cover. Simmer over gentle heat for 10 minutes, or until cooked. Don't allow the water to boil—it should gently simmer, to poach the chicken. Remove the chicken and allow to cool completely. Thinly slice the chicken.

To make the dressing, mix together the fish sauce, rice wine vinegar, lime juice and sugar.

Using a potato peeler, peel the papaya, and discard the seeds. Cut the papaya flesh into thin strips. Mix gently in a bowl with the Vietnamese mint, coriander and sliced chilli.

Arrange the papaya mixture on a serving plate and pile the sliced chicken on top. Scatter the peanuts over the top. Drizzle with the dressing, just before serving.

note   *Green papaya is underripe papaya, used for tartness and texture.*

pacific chicken salad

250 ml (9 fl oz/1 cup) coconut milk
1 tablespoon fish sauce
1 tablespoon grated palm (jaggery) sugar
(see Note)
4 boneless, skinless chicken breasts
2 mangoes, thinly sliced
4 spring onions (scallions), sliced
1 handful coriander (cilantro) leaves
45 g (1½ oz/⅓ cup) coarsely chopped
roasted unsalted macadamia nuts

dressing

2 tablespoons oil
1 teaspoon finely grated lime zest
2 tablespoons lime juice

serves 4

method Place the coconut milk, fish sauce and palm sugar in a frying pan and bring to the boil, stirring. Reduce the heat, add the chicken and gently simmer, covered, for 10 minutes, until the chicken is just tender and cooked through. Leave to cool in the coconut liquid, then remove and pour the liquid into a bowl.

To make the dressing, put 125 ml (4 fl oz/½ cup) of the reserved coconut liquid, the oil, lime zest and juice in a small bowl and whisk to combine. Season to taste with salt and freshly ground black pepper.

Cut each chicken breast diagonally into long slices and arrange with the sliced mango on individual serving plates, or in a large serving bowl. Spoon the dressing over the chicken and mango and top with the spring onion, coriander leaves and macadamia nuts.

note *Palm (jaggery) sugar is obtained from either the palmyra palm or sugar palm, and is available in block form or in jars. It can be grated or gently melted before using. Soft brown sugar may be substituted.*

red curry chicken salad

500 g (1 lb 2 oz) boneless, skinless chicken
 thighs, cut into thin strips
2 teaspoons Thai red curry paste
1 teaspoon chopped red chilli
1 garlic clove, crushed
1 stem lemongrass, white part only,
 finely chopped
cooking oil spray
1 red onion, thinly sliced
2 tomatoes, cut into wedges
2 tablespoons chopped mint
4 tablespoons chopped coriander
 (cilantro) leaves
400 g (14 oz) mixed salad leaves
2 tablespoons roasted peanuts

dressing

1½ tablespoons soft brown sugar
2 tablespoons fish sauce
2 tablespoons lime juice
2 makrut (kaffir lime) leaves, shredded
2 teaspoons oil

serves 4

method   Combine the chicken, red curry paste, chilli, garlic and lemongrass in a bowl. Cover and refrigerate overnight.

Lightly spray a non-stick frying pan with oil and cook the chicken in batches over medium–high heat for about 5–7 minutes until cooked through and lightly browned; set aside. Add the onion to the pan and cook for 3 minutes, or until just soft. Return the chicken and any juices to the pan and add the tomato, mint and coriander, stirring until heated. Set aside until just warm.

To make the dressing, put all the ingredients in a bowl and mix until well combined. In a bowl, toss the chicken mixture with the salad leaves and dressing. Sprinkle with the roasted peanuts, to serve.

italian-style chicken pasta salad

3 boneless, skinless chicken breasts
60 ml (2 fl oz/¼ cup) lemon juice
1 garlic clove, crushed
100 g (4 oz) thinly sliced prosciutto
1 Lebanese (short) cucumber
2 tablespoons seasoned pepper
2 tablespoons olive oil
135 g (5 oz/1½ cups) penne pasta, cooked
80 g (3 oz/½ cup) thinly sliced sun-dried
(sun-blushed) tomatoes
60 g (2 oz/½ cup) pitted black
olives, halved
110 g (4 oz/½ cup) halved bottled
artichoke hearts
parmesan cheese, shaved, to serve

creamy basil dressing

80 ml (3 fl oz/⅓ cup) olive oil
1 tablespoon white wine vinegar
¼ teaspoon seasoned pepper
1 teaspoon dijon mustard
3 teaspoons cornflour (cornstarch)
170 ml (6 fl oz/⅔ cup) cream

serves 6–8

method Remove the fat and sinew from the chicken. Flatten the chicken slightly with a mallet or rolling pin. Place the chicken in a non-metallic bowl with the combined lemon juice and garlic. Cover and refrigerate for at least 3 hours or overnight, turning occasionally.

Cut the prosciutto into strips. Halve the cucumber lengthways, then slice.

Drain the chicken and coat with the seasoned pepper. Heat the oil in a large heavy-based frying pan. Cook the chicken for 4 minutes on each side, or until lightly browned and cooked through. Remove from the heat and cool. Cut into pieces.

To make the dressing, combine the olive oil, vinegar, pepper and dijon mustard in a saucepan. Blend the cornflour with 80 ml (3 fl oz/⅓ cup) water until smooth, then add to the pan. Whisk over medium heat for 2 minutes, or until it boils and thickens. Add the cream, and salt to taste. Stir until heated.

Combine the pasta, chicken, cucumber, prosciutto, tomato, olives and artichokes in a serving bowl. Pour in the dressing and toss gently to combine. Serve warm or cold, sprinkled with the parmesan.

warm chicken salad

2 teaspoons cumin seeds
1 tablespoon olive oil
1 red onion, thinly sliced
3 garlic cloves, finely chopped
2 teaspoons finely chopped red chilli
1½ teaspoons sweet paprika
3 boneless, skinless chicken breasts, cut into
   bite-sized pieces
2 tablespoons lemon juice
2 tablespoons chopped coriander (cilantro)
   leaves
200 g (7 oz) mixed salad leaves
2 Lebanese (short) cucumbers, thinly sliced
12 Kalamata olives
2 tablespoons extra virgin olive oil

serves 4

method Dry-fry the cumin seeds in a frying pan for 1–2 minutes, or until fragrant. Remove and set aside. Heat the olive oil in the frying pan, add the onion and cook over medium heat until soft.

Add the garlic, cumin seeds, chopped chilli and paprika. Cook, stirring, for 1 minute. Add the chicken and cook, stirring, for 5 minutes, or until cooked through.

Remove from the heat and cool slightly. Stir in the lemon juice and coriander, and season to taste with salt. Arrange the salad leaves, cucumber and olives on a serving platter, drizzle with the extra virgin olive oil and place the chicken mixture on top. Serve immediately.

chicken and watercress salad

3 boneless, skinless chicken breasts
1 Lebanese (short) cucumber
½ red capsicum (pepper)
150 g (5 oz) watercress
1 small handful mint
2 tablespoons crisp-fried onion (see Note)

dressing

60 ml (2 fl oz/¼ cup) lime juice
2 tablespoons coconut milk
1 tablespoon fish sauce
1 tablespoon sweet chilli sauce

serves 4

method Line a bamboo steamer with baking paper and steam the chicken, covered, over a wok or saucepan of simmering water, for 10 minutes, or until the chicken is cooked through. Remove from the heat and set aside to cool. Thinly slice the cucumber and cut the slices in half. Slice the capsicum into thin strips.

While the chicken is cooling, pick over the watercress and separate the sprigs from the tough stems. Arrange the watercress and whole mint leaves on a serving plate. Using your fingers, tear the chicken into long, thin shreds. Gently toss the shredded chicken, cucumber and capsicum in a bowl. Arrange over the watercress bed.

To make the dressing, whisk all the ingredients until combined. Arrange the salad on a plate, sprinkle with the crisp-fried onion and drizzle with the dressing, just before serving.

note *Crisp-fried, or sometimes deep-fried, onions are available from Asian supermarkets.*

pasta

chicken ravioli

pasta

250 g (9 oz/2 cups) plain (all-purpose) flour
3 eggs
1 tablespoon olive oil
1 egg yolk, extra

filling

125 g (5 oz) minced (ground) chicken
75 g (3 oz) ricotta or cottage cheese
2 tablespoons grated parmesan cheese
60 g (2 oz) chicken livers, trimmed and
    chopped
30 g (1 oz) prosciutto, chopped
1 slice salami, chopped
1 egg, beaten
1 tablespoon chopped parsley
1 garlic clove, crushed
1/4 teaspoon mixed spice

tomato sauce

2 tablespoons olive oil
1 onion, finely chopped
2 garlic cloves, crushed
2 x 425 g (15 oz) tinned chopped tomatoes
1 handful chopped basil
1/2 teaspoon mixed herbs

serves 4

method   To make the pasta, sift the flour and a pinch of salt onto a board and make a well in the centre. Whisk together the eggs, oil and 1 tablespoon water. Add the egg mixture gradually to the flour, working in with your hands until the mixture forms a ball. Knead on a floured surface for 5 minutes, or until smooth and elastic. Place in a lightly oiled bowl, cover with plastic wrap and stand for 30 minutes.

To make the filling, put all the ingredients in a food processor and process until finely chopped. Season to taste with salt and freshly ground black pepper.

To make the sauce, heat the oil in a saucepan. Add the onion and garlic and stir over low heat until the onion is tender. Increase the heat, stir in the undrained tomatoes, basil, mixed herbs and season with salt and pepper. Bring to the boil. Reduce the heat and simmer for 15 minutes. Remove from the heat.

Roll out half the pasta dough until 2 mm (1/16 inch) thick. Cut with a knife or fluted pastry cutter into 10 cm (4 inch) strips. Place teaspoons of the filling at 5 cm (2 inch) intervals down one side of each strip. Whisk together the extra egg yolk and 60 ml (2 fl oz/1/4 cup) water. Brush along one side of the dough and between the filling. Fold the dough over the filling to meet the other side, then repeat with the remaining filling and dough. Press the edges of the dough firmly together to seal. Cut between the mounds of filling with a knife or a fluted pastry cutter.

Cook the ravioli in batches in a large saucepan of rapidly boiling water for 10 minutes each batch. Reheat the tomato sauce in a saucepan. Serve the sauce with the ravioli.

fettuccine with chicken and mushroom sauce

2 boneless, skinless chicken breasts
1 tablespoon olive oil
30 g (1 oz) butter
2 bacon slices, cut into thin strips
2 garlic cloves, crushed
250 g (9 oz) button mushrooms, sliced
80 ml (3 fl oz/⅓ cup) dry white wine
170 ml (6 fl oz/⅔ cup) cream
4 spring onions (scallions), chopped
1 tablespoon plain (all-purpose) flour
400 g (14 oz) fettuccine
parmesan cheese shavings, to serve

serves 4

method Trim the chicken of excess fat and sinew, and cut into strips. Heat the oil and butter in a heavy-based frying pan. Add the chicken strips and cook over medium heat for 3 minutes, or until browned. Add the bacon, garlic and mushrooms and cook over medium–high heat for 2 minutes, stirring occasionally.

Add the wine and cook until the liquid has reduced by half. Add the cream and spring onion, and bring to the boil. Blend the flour with 2 tablespoons water until smooth. Add to the pan and stir over the heat until the mixture boils and thickens, then reduce the heat and simmer for 2 minutes. Season to taste and keep warm.

Cook the fettuccine in a large saucepan of rapidly boiling water until al dente. Pour the sauce over the fettuccine and sprinkle with parmesan cheese. Serve immediately with herb bread on the side.

spaghetti with chicken meatballs

500 g (1 lb 2 oz) minced (ground) chicken
60 g (2 oz/heaped ½ cup) grated parmesan cheese
160 g (6 oz/2 cups) fresh white breadcrumbs
2 garlic cloves, crushed
1 egg
1 tablespoon chopped flat-leaf (Italian) parsley
1 tablespoon chopped sage
60 ml (2 fl oz/¼ cup) oil
500 g (1 lb 2 oz) spaghetti
2 tablespoons chopped oregano, to serve

tomato sauce

1 tablespoon olive oil
1 onion, finely chopped
2 kg (4 lb 8 oz) tomatoes, roughly chopped
2 bay leaves
1 large handful basil
1 teaspoon coarse ground black pepper

serves 4–6

method   In a large bowl, mix together the chicken, parmesan, breadcrumbs, garlic, egg, parsley, sage and some freshly ground black pepper. Shape tablespoons of the mixture into balls and chill for 30 minutes to firm. Heat the oil in a shallow frying pan and fry the meatballs in batches until golden brown, turning often by shaking the pan. Drain on paper towels.

To make the tomato sauce, heat the oil in a large saucepan, add the onion and fry for 1–2 minutes. Add the tomato and bay leaves, cover and bring to the boil, stirring occasionally. Reduce the heat to low, partially cover and cook for 50–60 minutes.

Add the meatballs, basil and pepper, and simmer, uncovered, for 10–15 minutes. Cook the spaghetti in boiling water until al dente. Drain, then return to the pan. Add some sauce to the pasta and toss gently to combine. Serve the pasta in individual bowls with the remaining sauce and the meatballs, sprinkled with fresh oregano.

chicken and pumpkin cannelloni

500 g (1 lb 2 oz) butternut pumpkin
(winter squash)
60 ml (2 fl oz/¼ cup) olive oil
100 g (4 oz) pancetta, roughly chopped
2 garlic cloves, crushed
500 g (1 lb 2 oz) minced (ground) chicken
½ teaspoon garam masala
2 tablespoons chopped flat-leaf (Italian) parsley
150 g (5 oz) goat's cheese
50 g (2 oz) ricotta cheese
375 g (13 oz) instant cannelloni tubes
100 g (4 oz/1 cup) grated parmesan cheese

tomato sauce

30 g (1 oz) butter
1 garlic clove, crushed
2 x 425 g (15 oz) tins chopped tomatoes
3 tablespoons chopped flat-leaf (Italian) parsley
60 ml (2 fl oz/¼ cup) white wine

serves 6

method   Preheat the oven to 220°C (425°F/Gas 7). Put the pumpkin on a baking tray. Brush with 1 tablespoon of the olive oil and bake for 40 minutes, or until tender. Scrape out the flesh of the cooked pumpkin and mash with a fork. Set aside to cool.

Add 1 tablespoon of the oil to a heavy-based frying pan and cook the pancetta over medium heat for 2–3 minutes. Remove from the pan and drain on paper towels.

In the same pan heat the remaining oil. Add the garlic and stir for 30 seconds. Add the chicken in small batches and brown, making sure the chicken is cooked through. Remove from the pan and drain on paper towels. Reduce the oven to 200°C (400°F/Gas 6).

Combine the pumpkin with the pancetta and chicken. Mix in the garam marsala, parsley, goat's cheese and ricotta. Season. Fill a cannelloni tube with the chicken mixture. Repeat with the rest of the tubes and filling.

To make the tomato sauce, melt the butter in a heavy-based saucepan. Add the garlic and cook for 1 minute, then add the tomato and simmer over medium heat for 1 minute. Add the parsley and white wine, and simmer for another 5 minutes. Season with salt and freshly ground pepper, to taste.

Arrange the cannelloni tubes over a little of the tomato sauce on the base of a 3 litre (12 cup) capacity ovenproof dish. Spoon the remaining tomato sauce over the cannelloni and sprinkle with the parmesan. Bake for about 20–25 minutes, or until the cheese is golden.

chicken tortellini with tomato sauce

pasta

250 g (9 oz/2 cups) plain (all-purpose) flour
3 eggs
1 tablespoon olive oil

filling

20 g (1 oz) butter
80 g (3 oz) chicken breast, cubed
2 slices pancetta, chopped
50 g (2 oz/½ cup) grated parmesan cheese
½ teaspoon nutmeg
1 egg, lightly beaten

tomato sauce

80 ml (3 fl oz/⅓ cup) olive oil
1.5 kg (3 lb 5 oz) ripe tomatoes, peeled
   and chopped
3 tablespoons chopped oregano
50 g (2 oz/½ cup) grated parmesan cheese
100 g (4 oz) fresh bocconcini, thinly sliced,
   to serve

serves 4

method   To make the pasta, sift the flour and a pinch of salt and make a well in the centre. Whisk together the eggs, oil and 1 tablespoon water. Add the egg mixture gradually to the flour, mixing to a firm dough. Gather together into a ball, adding a little extra water if necessary. Knead on a floured surface for
5 minutes, or until the dough is smooth. Place in a lightly oiled bowl and cover. Leave for 30 minutes.

To make the filling, heat the butter in a frying pan, add the chicken and cook until golden brown, then drain. Process the chicken and pancetta in a food processor until finely chopped. Transer to a bowl and add the parmesan, nutmeg, egg and salt and freshly ground pepper, to taste.

Roll out the dough very thinly on a lightly floured surface. Using a floured cutter, cut into 5 cm (2 inch) rounds. Spoon about ½ teaspoon of filling into the centre of each round. Fold the rounds in half to form semi-circles, pressing the edges together firmly. Wrap each semi-circle around your finger to form a ring and then press the ends of the dough together firmly.

To make the tomato sauce, put the oil, tomato and oregano in a frying pan and cook over medium–high heat for 10 minutes. Stir in the parmesan.

Cook the tortellini in two batches in rapidly boiling water for about 6 minutes each batch, or until al dente. Drain well and return to the pan. Reheat the tomato sauce. Divide the tortellini among bowls, top with tomato sauce and bocconcini and allow the cheese to melt a little before serving.

conchiglie with chicken and ricotta

500 g (1 lb 2 oz) conchiglie (shell pasta)
2 tablespoons olive oil
1 onion, chopped
1 garlic clove, crushed
60 g (2 oz) prosciutto, sliced
125 g (5 oz) mushrooms, chopped
250 g (9 oz) minced (ground) chicken
2 tablespoons tomato paste
(concentrated purée)
425 g (15 oz) tinned chopped tomatoes
125 ml (4 fl oz/½ cup) dry white wine
1 teaspoon dried oregano
250 g (9 oz) ricotta cheese
150 g (5 oz/1 cup) grated mozzarella cheese
1 teaspoon snipped chives
1 tablespoon chopped flat-leaf
(Italian) parsley
30 g (1 oz/¼ cup) grated parmesan cheese

serves 4

method   Add the conchiglie to a large saucepan of rapidly boiling water and cook until al dente. Drain well. Heat the oil in a large frying pan. Add the onion and garlic and stir over low heat until the onion is tender. Add the prosciutto and stir for 1 minute.

Add the mushrooms to the pan and cook for 2 minutes. Add the chicken and brown well, breaking up any lumps with a fork as it cooks. Stir in the tomato paste, undrained tomatoes, wine, oregano, salt and pepper. Bring to the boil, then reduce the heat and simmer for 20 minutes.

Preheat the oven to 180°C (350°F/Gas 4). Combine the ricotta, mozzarella, chives, parsley and half the grated parmesan. Spoon a little of the mixture into each pasta shell. Spoon some of the chicken sauce into the base of a casserole dish. Arrange the conchiglie on top and then spread the remaining sauce over the top. Sprinkle with the remaining parmesan and bake for 25–30 minutes, or until golden.

chicken ravioli with fresh tomato sauce

tomato sauce

1 tablespoon oil
1 large onion, chopped
2 garlic cloves, crushed
90 g (3 oz/⅓ cup) tomato paste
    (concentrated purée)
60 ml (2 fl oz/¼ cup) red wine
170 ml (6 fl oz/⅔ cup) chicken stock
2 tomatoes, chopped
1 tablespoon chopped basil

ravioli

200 g (7 oz) minced (ground) chicken
1 tablespoon chopped basil
30 g (1 oz/¼ cup) grated parmesan cheese
3 spring onions (scallions), finely chopped
50 g (2 oz) ricotta cheese
250 g (9 oz) packet (48) round won ton
    or gow gee wrappers

serves 4

method To make the tomato sauce, heat the oil in a saucepan and add the onion and garlic. Cook for 2–3 minutes, then stir in the tomato paste, wine, stock and tomato, and simmer for 20 minutes. Stir in the basil, and season with salt and freshly ground black pepper.

To make the ravioli, combine the chicken, basil, parmesan, spring onion, ricotta and some salt and pepper. Lay half of the wrappers on a flat surface and brush with a little water. Place slightly heaped teaspoons of the mixture onto the centre of each wrapper. Place another wrapper on top and press the edges firmly together to seal.

Bring a large saucepan of water to the boil. Add the ravioli, a few at a time, and cook for 2–3 minutes, or until just tender. Drain well and serve with the tomato sauce.

100 EASY RECIPES CHICKEN

spaghetti with chicken bolognaise

2 tablespoons olive oil
2 leeks, trimmed, thinly sliced
1 red capsicum (pepper), finely chopped
2 garlic cloves, crushed
500 g (1 lb 2 oz) minced (ground) chicken
500 g (1 lb 2 oz/2 cups) tomato passata
(puréed tomatoes)
1 tablespoon chopped thyme
1 tablespoon chopped rosemary
2 tablespoons pitted and chopped
black olives
400 g (14 oz) spaghetti
125 g (5 oz) feta cheese, crumbled
thyme sprigs, to serve

serves 4

method   Heat the oil in a large, heavy-based frying pan. Add the leek, capsicum and garlic and cook over medium–high heat for 2 minutes, or until lightly browned.

Add the chicken and cook over high heat for 3 minutes, until browned and any liquid has evaporated. Stir occasionally to break up any lumps as the chicken cooks.

Add the tomato passata, thyme and rosemary. Bring to the boil, then reduce the heat and simmer, uncovered, for 5 minutes, or until the sauce has reduced and thickened. Stir in the olives. Season with salt and freshly ground pepper.

Meanwhile, cook the spaghetti in a large saucepan of rapidly boiling water until al dente; drain. Place the spaghetti on individual serving plates or pile into a large deep serving dish and pour the chicken mixture over the top. Sprinkle with the feta and thyme and serve immediately.

variation   *Any type of pasta, dried or fresh, is suitable to use. Freshly grated parmesan or pecorino cheese can be used instead of feta.*

tagliatelle with chicken livers and cream

1 onion
300 g (11 oz) chicken livers
2 tablespoons olive oil
1 garlic clove, crushed
250 ml (9 fl oz/1 cup) cream
1 tablespoon snipped chives
1 teaspoon wholegrain mustard
2 eggs, beaten
375 g (13 oz) tagliatelle pasta
2 tablespoons shaved parmesan cheese,
   to serve
snipped chives, extra to serve

serves 4

method Chop the onion finely. Trim the chicken livers and chop them into small pieces.

Heat the oil in a large frying pan. Add the onion and garlic and stir over low heat until the onion is tender. Add the chicken livers to the pan. Cook gently for 2–3 minutes. Remove from the heat and stir in the cream, chives, mustard and salt and pepper, to taste. Return to the heat and bring to the boil. Add the egg and stir quickly to combine. Remove from the heat.

While the sauce is cooking, add the tagliatelle to a large saucepan of rapidly boiling water and cook until al dente. Drain well and return to the pan. Add the sauce to the hot pasta and toss to combine. Serve in warmed pasta bowls and sprinkle with the parmesan cheese and chives.

hint *Snip the chives with kitchen scissors.*

chicken and vegetable lasagne

500 g (1 lb 2 oz) boneless, skinless
chicken breasts
cooking oil spray
2 garlic cloves, crushed
1 onion, chopped
2 zucchini (courgettes), chopped
2 celery stalks, chopped
2 carrots, chopped
300 g (11 oz) pumpkin (winter squash), diced
2 x 400 g (14 oz) tinned chopped tomatoes
2 thyme sprigs
2 bay leaves
125 ml (4 fl oz/½ cup) white wine
2 tablespoons tomato paste
(concentrated purée)
2 tablespoons chopped basil
500 g (1 lb 2 oz) English spinach
500 g (1 lb 2 oz) reduced-fat cottage cheese
450 g (1 lb) ricotta cheese
60 ml (2 fl oz/¼ cup) skim milk
½ teaspoon ground nutmeg
300 g (11 oz) instant or fresh lasagne sheets
30 g (1 oz/¼ cup) grated parmesan cheese

serves 8

method   Preheat the oven to 180°C (350°F/Gas 4). Trim any excess fat from the chicken breasts, then finely mince in a food processor. Heat a large, deep, non-stick frying pan, spray with oil and cook the chicken in batches until browned. Remove and set aside.

Add the garlic and onion to the pan and cook until softened. Return the chicken to the pan and add the zucchini, celery, carrot, pumpkin, tomato, thyme, bay leaves, wine and tomato paste. Simmer, covered, for 20 minutes. Remove the bay leaves and thyme, stir in the basil and set aside.

Shred the spinach and set aside. Mix the cottage and ricotta cheeses, skim milk, nutmeg and half the grated parmesan.

Spoon a little of the tomato mixture over the base of a large casserole dish and top with a single layer of lasagne sheets. Top with half the remaining tomato mixture, then the spinach and spoon over half the cheese mixture. Continue with another layer of lasagne sheets, the remaining tomato and another layer of lasagne sheets. Spread the remaining cheese mixture on top and sprinkle with the parmesan. Bake for 40–50 minutes, or until golden. The top may puff up slightly but will settle on standing.

stir-fried chicken and pasta

270 g (10 oz) jar sun-dried (sun-blushed)
   tomatoes in oil
3 chicken breasts, cut into thin strips
2 garlic cloves, crushed
125 ml (4 fl oz/½ cup) cream
2 tablespoons shredded basil
400 g (14 oz) penne pasta, cooked
2 tablespoons pine nuts, toasted

serves 4–6

method   Drain the sun-dried tomatoes, reserving the oil. Thinly slice the sun-dried tomatoes.

Heat a wok until very hot, add 1 tablespoon of the reserved oil and swirl it around to coat the side. Stir-fry the chicken strips in batches, adding more oil when necessary.

Return all the chicken strips to the wok and add the garlic, sun-dried tomatoes and cream. Simmer gently for 4–5 minutes.

Divide the pasta among serving bowls, top with the sauce and sprinkle with the basil and pine nuts.

chicken agnolotti with buttered sage sauce

500 g (1 lb 2 oz) fresh or dried chicken-filled
agnolotti or ravioli
60 g (2 oz) butter
4 spring onions (scallions), chopped
2 tablespoons chopped sage
30 g (1 oz/¼ cup) grated parmesan cheese
sage leaves, chopped, to serve

serves 4

method Add the pasta to a large saucepan of rapidly boiling water and cook until al dente. Drain the pasta, then return to the pan.

While the pasta is cooking, melt the butter in a heavy-based frying pan. Add the spring onion and sage, and stir for 2 minutes. Season with salt and ground black pepper.

Add the sauce to the pasta and toss well. Pour onto a warmed serving platter and sprinkle with the parmesan and sage. Serve immediately.

hint *Bite through a piece of pasta to test whether it is done.*

stir-fries and pan-fries

lemon chicken

3 boneless, skinless chicken breasts
1 egg white, lightly beaten
2 teaspoons cornflour (cornstarch)
¼ teaspoon grated fresh ginger
60 ml (2 fl oz/¼ cup) oil

lemon sauce

2 teaspoons cornflour (cornstarch)
1½ tablespoons caster (superfine) sugar
2 tablespoons lemon juice
185 ml (6 fl oz/¾ cup) chicken stock
2 teaspoons soy sauce
1 teaspoon dry sherry

serves 4

method Pat the chicken dry with paper towels. Cut the chicken on the diagonal into 1 cm (½ inch) wide strips. Combine the egg white, cornflour, ginger and ½ teaspoon of salt. Add the chicken, mixing well. Marinate in the refrigerator for 30 minutes.

Heat the oil in a wok or heavy-based frying pan, swirling to coat the side. Drain the chicken from the marinade and stir-fry over medium–high heat for 5 minutes or until just cooked but not browned. Place the chicken on a plate to keep warm while preparing the sauce. Carefully pour the excess oil from the wok and discard.

To make the lemon sauce, mix the cornflour with 2 tablespoons water to form a smooth paste. Add to the wok with the remaining ingredients. Stir over high heat and boil for 1 minute. Add the chicken, stirring to coat it with the sauce. Transfer to a serving platter. Serve immediately with steamed rice and stir-fried vegetables.

chicken chow mein

500 g (1 lb 2 oz) boneless, skinless chicken thighs, cut into small cubes
1½ tablespoon cornflour (cornstarch)
60 ml (2 fl oz/¼ cup) soy sauce
1 tablespoon oyster sauce
2 teaspoons sugar
oil, for cooking
2 onions, thinly sliced
2 garlic cloves, finely chopped
1 tablespoon finely chopped fresh ginger
1 green capsicum (pepper), cubed
2 celery stalks, diagonally sliced
8 spring onions (scallions), cut into short pieces
100 g (4 oz) mushrooms, thinly sliced
80 g (3 oz/½ cup) water chestnuts, thinly sliced
1 tablespoon dry sherry
125 ml (4 fl oz/½ cup) chicken stock
90 g (3 oz) Chinese cabbage, finely shredded
200 g (7 oz) ready-prepared fried noodles

serves 4–6

method   In a glass or ceramic bowl, combine the chicken cubes with 1 tablespoon of the cornflour, 2 tablespoons of the soy sauce, the oyster sauce and sugar. Cover and refrigerate for 1 hour.

Heat the wok until very hot, gradually add 1 tablespoon of the oil and swirl it around to coat the side. Stir-fry the chicken in two batches over high heat for 4–5 minutes, or until cooked. Add oil between batches. Remove all the chicken from the wok and set it aside.

Reheat the wok, add 1 tablespoon of the oil and stir-fry the onion slices over medium–high heat for 3–4 minutes, or until the onion is slightly softened. Add the garlic, ginger, capsicum, celery, spring onion, mushrooms and water chestnuts. Stir-fry over high heat for 3–4 minutes, or until tender.

Combine the remaining cornflour with the sherry, chicken stock and remaining soy sauce. Add to the wok and bring to the boil. Simmer for 1–2 minutes, or slightly thickened. Stir in the cabbage and cook, covered, for 1–2 minutes, or until the cabbage is just wilted. Return all the chicken to the wok and toss until heated through. Season to taste with salt and freshly ground pepper. Arrange the noodles around the edge of a large platter and spoon the chicken mixture into the centre. Serve immediately.

chicken biryani

marinade

6 cardamom pods
3 onions, finely chopped
3 garlic cloves, finely chopped
5 cm (2 inch) piece ginger, finely chopped
¼ teaspoon ground cloves
1 teaspoon ground black pepper
1 teaspoon ground cumin
1 teaspoon ground cinnamon
¼ teaspoon ground nutmeg
1½ tablespoons poppy seeds
2 tablespoons lemon juice
250 g (9 oz/1 cup) plain yoghurt

1 kg (2 lb 4 oz) chicken, cut into small pieces
80 ml (3 fl oz/⅓ cup) oil
3 bay leaves
2 whole cardamom pods, lightly crushed
3 onions, very thinly sliced
2 tablespoons raisins
300 g (11 oz/1½ cups) long-grain white rice
60 ml (2 fl oz/¼ cup) milk
1 teaspoon sugar
1 teaspoon saffron threads
plain yoghurt, to serve
40 g (1½ oz/¼ cup) toasted cashews,
    to serve

serves 6

method To make the marinade, crush the cardamom pods to release the seeds; discard the pods. Add the onions, garlic, ginger, spices, poppy seeds and lemon juice. Stir in the yoghurt and season with salt. Prick the skin of the chicken with a fork and place in a large non-metallic bowl. Add the marinade and evenly coat the chicken, then refrigerate for 4 hours, or overnight.

Heat 60 ml (2 fl oz/¼ cup) of the oil in a frying pan over low heat. Cook the bay leaves and cardamom pods for 2 minutes, without burning. Discard the bay leaves and cardamom. Add the onion and raisins and fry for 8 minutes, or until the onion is golden. Remove with a slotted spoon, reserving the oil.

Place the chicken and the marinade in a flameproof casserole dish and bring to the boil. Cover and simmer for 15 minutes. Remove the chicken with a slotted spoon, leaving as much marinade in the pan as possible. Cook the marinade until reduced to about 250 ml (9 fl oz/1 cup). Return the chicken and toss to coat in the thickened sauce. Set aside.

Add the rice to a large saucepan of boiling water and cook for 7 minutes. (Do not cook the rice until tender.) Drain the rice into a sieve. Meanwhile, heat the milk and sugar, pour into a bowl, add the saffron and soak for 5 minutes.

Preheat the oven to 150°C (300°F/Gas 2). Pour the saffron mixture over the rice and mix to combine, using a fork. Spoon the rice over the chicken. Pour over the reserved oil. Cover the dish tightly with foil and bake for 1 hour, until the rice and chicken are cooked through and tender. Sprinkle with the cashews and serve the yoghurt separately.

pan-fried chicken with vegetables

2 tablespoons olive oil
6 slices prosciutto, cut crossways into
thin strips
500 g (1 lb 2 oz) chicken tenderloins
1 red onion, chopped
2 garlic cloves, crushed
1 small red chilli, chopped
1 tablespoon plain (all-purpose) flour
375 ml (13 fl oz/1½ cups) chicken stock
150 g (5 oz) asparagus, halved
250 g (9 oz) green beans, halved
4 tablespoons snipped chives

serves 4

method Heat 1 tablespoon of the oil in a frying pan. Stir-fry the prosciutto over medium–high heat for 2 minutes, or until crisp. Lift out with a slotted spoon and drain on paper towels.

Add the chicken to the pan and cook over high heat for 2 minutes on each side, or until brown, turning once. Remove from the frying pan and drain on paper towels.

Heat the remaining oil in the frying pan. Add the onion, garlic and chilli and stir-fry over medium–high heat for 2 minutes, or until softened. Add the flour and stir for 1 minute.

Add the stock gradually, stirring over the heat until the mixture boils and thickens. Add the asparagus and beans and reduce the heat to low. Cook, covered, for 3–5 minutes, until the vegetables are tender. Return the chicken to the pan and cook for 4 minutes, until the chicken is cooked through. Stir in the snipped chives and serve hot. Sprinkle with the prosciutto.

hint *Serve this dish with penne pasta or steamed potatoes.*

sichuan pepper chicken stir-fry

3 teaspoons sichuan peppercorns
500 g (1 lb 2 oz) boneless, skinless chicken
thighs, cut into strips
2 tablespoons soy sauce
1 garlic clove, crushed
1 teaspoon grated fresh ginger
3 teaspoons cornflour (cornstarch)
100 g (4 oz) dried thin egg noodles
oil, for cooking
1 onion, sliced
1 yellow capsicum (pepper), cut into
thin strips
1 red capsicum (pepper), cut into thin strips
100 g (4 oz) sugar snap peas
60 ml (2 fl oz/¼ cup) chicken stock

serves 4

method   Heat a wok until very hot and dry-fry the sichuan peppercorns for 30 seconds. Remove from the wok and crush with a mortar and pestle or in a spice mill or small food processor. Combine the chicken with the soy sauce, garlic, ginger, cornflour and sichuan pepper in a glass or ceramic bowl. Cover and refrigerate for 2 hours.

Bring a large saucepan of water to the boil and cook the egg noodles for 5 minutes, or until tender. Drain, then drizzle with a little oil and toss it through the noodles to prevent them from sticking together. Set aside.

Heat the wok until very hot, add 1 tablespoon of the oil and swirl it around to coat the side. Stir-fry the chicken in batches over medium–high heat for 5 minutes, or until golden brown and cooked. Add more oil when necessary. Remove from the wok and set aside.

Reheat the wok, add 1 tablespoon of the oil and stir-fry the onion, capsicum and sugar snap peas over high heat for 2–3 minutes, or until the vegetables are tender. Add the chicken stock and bring to the boil. Return the chicken and egg noodles to the wok and toss over high heat until the mixture is well combined. Serve immediately.

chicken and cashew stir-fry

oil, for cooking
750 g (1 lb 10 oz) boneless, skinless chicken
thighs, cut into strips
2 egg whites, lightly beaten
60 g (2 oz/½ cup) cornflour (cornstarch)
2 onions, thinly sliced
1 red capsicum (pepper), thinly sliced
200 g (7 oz) broccoli, cut into
bite-sized pieces
2 tablespoons soy sauce
2 tablespoons dry sherry
1 tablespoon oyster sauce
50 g (2 oz/⅓ cup) roasted cashews
4 spring onions (scallions), diagonally sliced

serves 4–6

method   Heat a wok until very hot, add 1 tablespoon of the oil and swirl it around to coat the side. Dip about a quarter of the chicken strips into the egg white and then into the cornflour. Add to the wok and stir-fry for 3–5 minutes, or until the chicken is golden brown and just cooked. Drain on paper towels and repeat with the remaining chicken, reheating the wok and adding a little more oil each time.

Reheat the wok, add 1 tablespoon of the oil and stir-fry the onion, capsicum and broccoli over medium heat for 4–5 minutes, or until the vegetables have softened slightly. Increase the heat to high and add the soy sauce, sherry and oyster sauce. Toss the vegetables well in the sauce and bring to the boil.

Return the chicken to the wok and toss over high heat for 1–2 minutes to heat the chicken and make sure it is entirely cooked through. Season well with salt and freshly cracked pepper. Toss the cashews and spring onion through the chicken mixture, and serve immediately.

rice with chicken and seafood

500 g (1 lb 2 oz) raw medium prawns
500 g (1 lb 2 oz) mussels
200 g (7 oz) squid tubes
60 ml (2 fl oz/¼ cup) olive oil
2 chorizo sausages, thickly sliced
500 g (1 lb 2 oz) chicken pieces
300 g (11 oz) pork fillet, thickly sliced
4 garlic cloves, crushed
2 red onions, chopped
¼ teaspoon saffron threads, soaked in
    hot water
¼ teaspoon turmeric
4 large tomatoes, peeled, seeded and
    chopped
440 g (15 oz/2 cups) short-grain rice
1.25 litres (5 cups) hot chicken stock
125 g (5 oz) green beans, cut into 4 cm
    (1½ inch) lengths
1 red capsicum (pepper), cut into thin strips
155 g (5 oz/1 cup) fresh peas, shelled

serves 4–6

method   Peel the prawns. Devein, leaving the tails intact. Scrub the mussels and remove the beards. Cut the squid tubes into 5 mm (¼ inch) thin slices. Heat 1 tablespoon of the oil in a large frying pan and add the chorizo. Cook over medium heat for 5 minutes, or until browned. Drain. Add the chicken pieces and cook for 5 minutes, or until golden, turning once. Drain.

Add the pork to the pan and cook for about 3 minutes, or until browned, turning once. Drain. Heat the remaining oil in the pan, add the garlic, onion, drained saffron and turmeric, cook over medium heat until the onion is soft. Add the tomato and cook for 3 minutes, or until soft.

Add the rice and stir until the rice is translucent. Stir in the hot stock and bring to the boil, then cover and simmer for 10 minutes. Add the chicken, cover and cook for 20 minutes. Add the pork, prawns, mussels, calamari, chorizo, beans, capsicum and peas. Cover and cook for 10 minutes, until the liquid has been absorbed.

stuffed chicken breast

80 ml (3 fl oz/⅓ cup) olive oil
1 onion, finely chopped
2 garlic cloves, crushed
100 g (4 oz) ham, finely chopped
1 green capsicum (pepper), finely chopped
2 tablespoons finely chopped pitted
black olives
35 g (1 oz/⅓ cup) grated parmesan cheese
6 boneless, skinless chicken breasts
plain (all-purpose) flour, to coat
2 eggs, lightly beaten
150 g (5 oz/1½ cups) dry breadcrumbs

serves 6

method Heat 1 tablespoon of the oil in a saucepan and add the onion, garlic, ham and capsicum. Cook, stirring, over medium heat for 5 minutes, or until the onion is soft. Transfer the mixture to a heatproof bowl. Add the olives and the parmesan cheese.

Cut a deep pocket in the side of each chicken breast, cutting almost through to the other side. Fill each chicken breast with the ham mixture and secure with toothpicks along the opening of the pocket. Coat each fillet with the flour, shaking off any excess, dip into the egg and then coat with the breadcrumbs.

Heat the remaining oil in a large frying pan and cook the chicken, in batches, over medium–high heat for 15–20 minutes, turning halfway through, until golden and cooked through. To serve, remove the toothpicks, then cut diagonally into thin slices.

chicken with oyster sauce and basil

60 ml (2 fl oz/¼ cup) oyster sauce
2 tablespoons fish sauce
1 tablespoon grated palm (jaggery) sugar
1 tablespoon oil
2–3 garlic cloves, crushed
1 tablespoon grated fresh ginger
1–2 red chillies, seeded and finely chopped
4 spring onions (scallions), finely chopped
1 boneless, skinless chicken breast, cut into
   thin strips
250 g (9 oz) broccoli, cut into florets
230 g (8 oz) tinned water chestnuts, drained
230 g (8 oz) tinned sliced bamboo
   shoots, rinsed
1 handful basil, shredded

serves 4

method Put 60 ml (2 fl oz/¼ cup) water in a bowl with the oyster sauce, fish sauce and palm sugar. Mix well.

Heat a wok until very hot, add the oil and swirl it around to coat the side. Stir-fry the garlic, ginger, chilli and spring onion for 1 minute over medium heat. Increase the heat to high, add the chicken and stir-fry for 2–3 minutes, or until it is just cooked. Remove from the wok.

Reheat the wok. Add the broccoli florets, water chestnuts and bamboo shoots. Stir-fry for 2–3 minutes, tossing constantly. Add the sauce and then bring to the boil, tossing constantly. Return the chicken to the wok and toss until it is heated through. Stir in the basil and serve immediately.

fried crispy noodles

100 g (4 oz) rice vermicelli
500 ml (17 fl oz/2 cups) oil, for deep-frying
100 g (4 oz) fried bean curd,
cut into matchsticks
2 garlic cloves, finely chopped
4 cm (1½ inch) piece ginger, grated
150 g (5 oz) minced (ground) chicken
100 g (4 oz) raw prawn (shrimp) meat,
finely chopped
1 tablespoon white vinegar
2 tablespoons fish sauce
2 tablespoons soft brown sugar
2 tablespoons chilli sauce
1 teaspoon chopped red chilli
2 small knobs pickled garlic, chopped
1 handful garlic chives, snipped
1 large handful coriander (cilantro) leaves

serves 4

method   Place the vermicelli in a bowl of hot water for 1 minute. Drain and allow to dry for 20 minutes. Heat the oil in a wok or deep frying pan, add the bean curd in two batches and cook for 1 minute, or until golden and crisp. Drain.

Add the completely dry vermicelli to the wok in several batches and cook for 10 seconds, or until puffed and crisp. Remove from the oil immediately to prevent the vermicelli absorbing too much oil. Drain on paper towels and allow to cool.

Drain all but 1 tablespoon of the oil from the wok. Reheat the wok over high heat. Add the garlic, ginger, chicken and prawn meat; stir-fry for 2 minutes, or until golden brown. Add the vinegar, fish sauce, brown sugar, chilli sauce and chilli, and stir until boiling.

Just before serving, add the noodles and bean curd to the wok and toss thoroughly. Quickly toss through the pickled garlic, chives and coriander. Serve immediately.

chicken pilaf with spices

1.5 kg (3 lb 5 oz) chicken pieces
80 ml (3 fl oz/⅓ cup) canola oil
40 g (1½ oz/¼ cup) unblanched
  whole almonds
2 onions, thinly sliced
3 garlic cloves garlic, crushed
1 teaspoon whole black peppercorns
1 teaspoon turmeric
1 teaspoon cumin seeds
2 bay leaves
5 whole cloves
1 cinnamon stick
440 g (15 oz/2¼ cups) long-grain rice
1 litre (35 fl oz/4 cups) chicken stock
80 g (3 oz/½ cup) fresh or frozen peas
30 g (1 oz/¼ cup) sultanas (golden raisins)
3 hard-boiled eggs, peeled and quartered
coriander (cilantro) leaves, to serve

serves 4

method   Trim the chicken of excess fat and sinew. Heat half the oil in a large frying pan. Add the chicken pieces in batches and cook over medium heat for 5–10 minutes, or until the chicken is brown all over. Drain. Heat 1 tablespoon of the oil in a pan. Add the almonds and cook until the nuts are brown. Remove from the pan and set aside.

Heat the remaining oil in a large frying pan. Add the onion and garlic and cook gently over low heat for 2 minutes, stirring occasionally. Add the peppercorns, turmeric, cumin, bay leaves, cloves and cinnamon stick. Fry over high heat for 1 minute, or until fragrant. Stir in the rice, making sure it is well coated with the spices.

Add the stock, browned chicken pieces and salt to taste. Bring to the boil, reduce the heat and simmer, covered, for 20 minutes. Add the peas and sultanas and simmer for a further 5 minutes, or until all the liquid is absorbed and the chicken is cooked (you may need to add extra stock or water). Serve with the hard-boiled eggs and sprinkle with the almonds and coriander.

curried rice noodles with chicken

200 g (7 oz) thin rice stick noodles
1½ tablespoons oil
1 tablespoon red curry paste
3 boneless, skinless chicken thighs, cut into thin strips
1–2 teaspoons chopped red chilli
2 tablespoons fish sauce
2 tablespoons lime juice
100 g (4 oz) bean sprouts
80 g (3 oz/½ cup) chopped roasted peanuts
2 tablespoons crisp-fried onion
2 tablespoons crisp-fried garlic
1 large handful coriander (cilantro) leaves

serves 4–6

method   Cook the noodles in a saucepan of rapidly boiling water for 2 minutes. Drain and then toss with 2 teaspoons of the oil to prevent the strands from sticking together. Set aside.

Heat the remaining oil in a wok, add the curry paste and stir for 1 minute, or until the paste is fragrant. Add the chicken in batches and stir-fry for 2 minutes, or until golden brown. Return all of the chicken to the pan.

Add the chopped chilli, fish sauce and lime juice. Bring to the boil and simmer for 1 minute. Add the bean sprouts and noodles and toss well. Arrange the noodles on a plate and sprinkle with the peanuts, onion, garlic and coriander leaves. Serve immediately.

goan-style chicken with almonds

2 teaspoons ground cumin
2 teaspoons ground coriander
1 teaspoon ground cinnamon
½ teaspoon cayenne pepper
½ teaspoon ground cardamom
oil, for cooking
1 large onion, cut into thin wedges
2 garlic cloves, finely chopped
500 g (1 lb 2 oz) boneless, skinless chicken
    breasts, cut into cubes
2 teaspoons finely grated orange zest
2 tablespoons orange juice
2 tablespoons sultanas (golden raisins)
1 teaspoon soft brown sugar
60 g (2 oz/¼ cup) thick plain yoghurt
40 g (1½ oz/⅓ cup) slivered almonds, toasted

serves 3–4

method Dry-fry the spices in a wok over low heat for about 1 minute, or until fragrant, shaking the wok regularly.

Add 1 tablespoon oil to the wok and stir-fry the onion wedges and garlic over high heat for 3 minutes. Remove from the wok.

Reheat the wok, add 1 tablespoon of the oil and stir-fry the chicken in two batches until golden and just cooked. Return all the chicken to the wok with the onion mixture, orange zest, juice, sultanas and sugar. Cook for 1 minute, tossing until most of the juice evaporates.

Stir in the yoghurt and reheat gently, without boiling or the yoghurt will separate. Season well with salt and pepper. Serve garnished with the toasted almonds.

note *Yoghurt separates easily when heated due to its acid balance. Yoghurt also separates when shaken, whipped or stirred too much.*

100 EASY RECIPES CHICKEN

honey chicken

oil, for cooking
500 g (1 lb 2 oz) boneless, skinless chicken
thighs, cut into cubes
1 egg white, lightly beaten
40 g (1 ½ oz/⅓ cup) cornflour (cornstarch)
2 onions, thinly sliced
1 green capsicum (pepper), cubed
2 carrots, cut into matchsticks
100 g (4 oz) snow peas (mangetouts), sliced
90 g (3 oz/¼ cup) honey
2 tablespoons toasted almonds

serves 4

method   Heat a wok until very hot, gradually add 1½ tablespoons of the oil and swirl it around to coat the side. Dip half of the chicken into the egg white, then lightly dust it with the cornflour. Stir-fry over high heat for 4–5 minutes, or until the chicken is golden brown and just cooked. Remove from the wok and drain on paper towels. Repeat with the remaining chicken, then remove all the chicken from the wok.

Reheat the wok, add 1 tablespoon of the oil and stir-fry the sliced onion over high heat for 3–4 minutes, or until slightly softened. Add the capsicum and carrot, and cook, tossing, for 3–4 minutes, or until just tender. Stir in the snow peas and cook for 2 minutes.

Increase the heat, add the honey and toss the vegetables until well coated. Return the chicken to the wok and toss until it is heated through and is well coated in the honey. Remove from the heat and season to taste with salt and pepper. Serve immediately, sprinkled with the almonds.

chicken with olives and sun-dried tomatoes

olive oil, for cooking
4 boneless, skinless chicken breasts, cut
   diagonally into thin slices
1 red onion, thinly sliced
3 garlic cloves, finely chopped
2 tablespoons white wine vinegar
1 teaspoon sambal oelek
1 tablespoon lemon juice
12 Kalamata olives, pitted and quartered
   lengthways
40 g (1½ oz/¼ cup) sun-dried tomatoes,
   cut into thin strips
1 tablespoon shredded basil

serves 4

method   Heat a wok until very hot, add 2 teaspoons of the oil and swirl to coat the side. Stir-fry the chicken slices in two batches until browned and cooked through, adding more oil in between each batch. Remove all the chicken from the wok and keep warm.

Reheat the wok, add 1 tablespoon of the oil and stir-fry the onion until it is soft and golden. Add the garlic and cook for 1 minute. Return the warm chicken to the wok. Add the vinegar, sambal oelek and lemon juice, and toss well.

Stir in the olive pieces, sun-dried tomato and basil, and season with salt and ground black pepper. Heat through thoroughly.

nasi goreng

5–8 long red chillies, seeded and chopped
2 teaspoons shrimp paste
8 garlic cloves, finely chopped
oil, for cooking
2 eggs, lightly beaten
350 g (12 oz) boneless, skinless chicken thighs,
cut into thin strips
200 g (7 oz) peeled raw prawns (shrimps),
deveined
1.5 kg (3 lb 5 oz/8 cups) cooked rice
80 ml (3 fl oz/⅓ cup) kecap manis
80 ml (3 fl oz/⅓ cup) soy sauce
2 small Lebanese (short) cucumbers,
finely chopped
1 large tomato, finely chopped
lime wedges, to serve

serves 4–6

method Mix the red chilli, shrimp paste and chopped garlic in a food processor until the mixture resembles a paste.

Heat a wok until very hot, add 1 tablespoon oil and swirl it around to coat the side. Add the beaten egg and, using a metal spatula, push the egg up the edges of the wok to form a large omelette. Cook for 1 minute over medium heat, or until the egg is set, then flip it over and cook the other side for 1 minute. Remove from the wok and cool before slicing into strips.

Reheat the wok, add 1 tablespoon oil and stir-fry the chicken and half the chilli paste over high heat for about 4 minutes or until the chicken is just cooked. Remove the chicken from the wok.

Reheat the wok, add 1 tablespoon oil and stir-fry the prawns and the remaining chilli paste for about 3–4 minutes until the prawns are cooked. Remove the prawns from the wok and set aside.

Reheat the wok, add 1 tablespoon oil and the cooked rice, and toss constantly over medium heat for 4–5 minutes, or until the rice is heated through. Add the kecap manis and soy sauce, and toss until all of the rice is coated in the sauces. Return the chicken and prawns to the wok, and toss until well combined and heated through. Season to taste with salt and pepper. Transfer to a large deep serving bowl and top with the omelette strips, cucumber and tomato. Serve with the lime wedges.

chicken donburi

440 g (15 oz/2 cups) short-grain rice
2 tablespoons oil
250 g (9 oz) boneless, skinless chicken breasts, cut into thin strips
2 onions, thinly sliced
80 ml (3 fl oz/⅓ cup) shoyu (Japanese soy sauce)
2 tablespoons mirin
1 teaspoon dashi granules
5 eggs, lightly beaten
2 nori sheets
2 spring onions (scallions), sliced

serves 4

method Wash the rice in a colander under cold running water until the water runs clear. Transfer the rice to a heavy-based saucepan, add 600 ml (21 fl oz) water and bring to the boil over high heat. Cover the pan with a tight-fitting lid and reduce the heat to as low as possible and cook for 15 minutes. Turn the heat to very high, for 15–20 seconds, then remove from the heat and set aside for 12 minutes, without lifting the lid or the steam will escape.

Heat the oil in a frying pan over high heat. Add the chicken strips and stir-fry until tender. Remove the chicken from the pan and set aside. Reheat the pan, add the onion and cook, stirring occasionally, for 3 minutes, or until beginning to soften. Add 80 ml (3 fl oz/⅓ cup) water, the shoyu, mirin and dashi granules. Stir to dissolve the dashi, and bring to the boil. Cook for 3 minutes, until the onion is tender.

Return the chicken to the pan and pour in the egg, stirring gently to break up. Cover and simmer over very low heat for 2–3 minutes, or until the egg is just set. Remove the pan from the heat. To make the nori crisp, hold it over low heat, moving it back and forward for about 15 seconds, then crumble it into small pieces.

Transfer the rice to a serving dish, carefully spoon over the chicken and egg mixture and sprinkle with the crumbled nori. Garnish with the spring onion.

100 EASY RECIPES CHICKEN

chiang mai noodles

500 g (1 lb 2 oz) fresh egg noodles
1 tablespoon oil
3 red Asian or French shallots (eschalots),
peeled and chopped
6 garlic cloves, chopped
2 teaspoons finely chopped red chilli, optional
1–2 tablespoons red curry paste
350 g (12 oz) boneless, skinless chicken breast,
thinly sliced
1 carrot, cut into fine, thin strips
2 tablespoons fish sauce
2 teaspoons soft brown sugar
3 spring onions (scallions), thinly sliced
1 small handful coriander (cilantro) leaves

serves 4

method   Cook the noodles in a wok or saucepan of rapidly boiling water for 2–3 minutes, or until they are just tender. Drain and keep warm.

Heat the oil in a wok or large frying pan until very hot. Add the shallots, garlic, chilli and curry paste, and stir-fry for 2 minutes, or until the mixture is fragrant. Add the chicken in two batches and cook for 3 minutes, or until the chicken changes colour.

Return all of the chicken to the wok. Add the carrot, fish sauce and brown sugar, and bring to the boil. Divide the noodles between serving bowls and mix in portions of the chicken mixture and spring onion. Top with the coriander leaves. Serve immediately.

hint   *This dish must be served as soon as it is cooked or the noodles and vegetables will go soggy.*

grills and barbecues

chicken burger with tangy garlic mayonnaise

4 boneless, skinless chicken breasts
125 ml (4 fl oz/½ cup) lime juice
1 tablespoon sweet chilli sauce
4 bacon slices
4 hamburger buns, halved
4 lettuce leaves
1 large tomato, sliced

garlic mayonnaise

2 egg yolks
2 garlic cloves, crushed
1 tablespoon dijon mustard
1 tablespoon lemon juice
125 ml (4 fl oz/½ cup) olive oil

serves 4

method   Put the chicken in a shallow non-metallic dish and prick several times with a skewer. Combine the lime juice and sweet chilli sauce in a bowl. Pour over the chicken, cover and refrigerate for several hours or overnight.

To make the mayonnaise, place the egg yolks, garlic, mustard and lemon juice in a food processor or blender and process until smooth. With the motor running, add the oil in a thin, steady stream. Process until the mixture reaches a thick consistency. Refrigerate, covered, until required.

Preheat a barbecue grill or flatplate to high. Remove and discard the rind from the bacon, and cut the bacon in half crossways. Lightly grease the hot barbecue. Cook the chicken and bacon for 5 minutes, or until crisp. Cook the chicken for a further 5–10 minutes, or until well browned and cooked through, turning once.

Toast the hamburger buns until lightly browned. Arrange the lettuce, tomato, chicken and bacon on the bases. Top with the garlic mayonnaise and finish with the remaining bun top.

honey-glazed chicken breasts

6 boneless, skinless chicken breasts
50 g (2 oz) butter, softened
90 g (3 oz/¼ cup) honey
60 ml (2 fl oz/¼ cup) barbecue sauce
2 teaspoons wholegrain mustard

serves 6

method   Trim the chicken of any excess fat and sinew. Using a sharp knife, make three or four diagonal cuts across one side of each chicken breast. Preheat a barbecue grill or flatplate to high.

Combine the butter, honey, barbecue sauce and mustard in a small bowl. Spread half of the honey mixture thickly over the slashed side of the chicken. Cover with plastic wrap and stand at room temperature for 20 minutes. Set the remaining honey mixture aside.

Lightly grease the hot barbecue grill or flatplate. Cook the chicken breasts, slashed side up first, for 2–3 minutes each side, or until the chicken is cooked through and tender. Brush with the reserved honey mixture several times during cooking. Serve with a mixed salad.

notes   *Barbecue the chicken just before serving. The chicken can be marinated overnight in the refrigerator. When honey is cooked, its sugars caramelise and some of its flavour is lost. For a distinctive taste to this dish, use a dark honey with a strong flavour, such as leatherwood, lavender or rosemary. Lighter honeys, such as yellow box, orange blossom or clover, will sweeten and glaze the meat without necessarily affecting its flavour. Usually the paler the honey, the milder its flavour.*

buffalo wings with ranch dressing

8 large chicken wings
2 teaspoons black pepper
2 teaspoons garlic salt
2 teaspoons onion powder
olive oil, for deep-frying
125 ml (4 fl oz/½ cup) tomato
    sauce (ketchup)
2 tablespoons worcestershire sauce
20 g (1 oz) butter, melted
2 teaspoons sugar
Tabasco sauce, to taste

ranch dressing

125 g (5 oz/½ cup) whole-egg mayonnaise
125 g (5 oz/½ cup) sour cream
2 tablespoons lemon juice
2 tablespoons snipped chives

serves 4

method Pat the chicken wings dry with paper towels. Cut the tips off each wing and discard. Bend each wing back to snap the joint, and cut through to create two pieces. Combine the pepper, garlic salt and onion powder. Rub into each chicken piece.

Heat the oil to moderately hot in a deep heavy-based frying pan. Cook the chicken pieces in batches for 2 minutes. Remove and drain on paper towels.

Put the chicken in a non-metallic bowl or shallow dish. Combine the sauces, butter, sugar and Tabasco. Pour the mixture over the chicken and stir to coat. Refrigerate, covered, for several hours or overnight.

To make the ranch dressing, combine the mayonnaise, sour cream, lemon juice, chives, salt and white pepper in a bowl and mix well.

Preheat a barbecue grill or flat plate to high. Lightly oil the barbecue. Cook the chicken for 5 minutes, turning and brushing with the marinade. Serve with the dressing.

100 EASY RECIPES CHICKEN

tandoori barbecue chicken

4 chicken leg quarters (marylands), skin removed
1 teaspoon salt
2 garlic cloves, crushed
1 tablespoon lemon juice
250 g (9 oz/1 cup) plain yoghurt
1½ teaspoons garam masala
½ teaspoon ground black pepper
½ teaspoon ground turmeric
2–3 drops red food colouring
20–30 mesquite or hickory chips, for smoking
olive oil, for basting

serves 4

method   Place the chicken in a large non-metallic dish and rub with the salt and garlic. Combine the lemon juice, yoghurt, garam masala, pepper and turmeric in a bowl. Add enough food colouring to make the marinade a bright orange–red colour. Pour over the chicken and coat with the back of a spoon. Refrigerate, covered, for 4 hours, turning the chicken every hour.

Prepare a kettle barbecue for indirect cooking. When the barbecue coals are covered with fine white ash, add the mesquite or hickory chips to the coals. Cover the barbecue and leave until the smoke is well established (about 5 minutes).

Brush the barbecue grill with oil. Arrange the chicken on the grill and put the lid on the barbecue. Smoke-cook for 45 minutes–1 hour, or until the chicken is well crisped. Brush the chicken with the oil several times during cooking.

chargrilled chicken

4 boneless, skinless chicken breasts
2 tablespoons honey
1 tablespoon wholegrain mustard
1 tablespoon soy sauce
2 red onions, cut into wedges
8 roma (plum) tomatoes, halved lengthways
2 tablespoons soft brown sugar
2 tablespoons balsamic vinegar
cooking oil spray
1 tablespoon basil, for serving

serves 4

method   Preheat the oven to 180°C (350°F/Gas 4). Trim the chicken of any excess fat and place in a shallow dish. Combine the honey, mustard and soy sauce and pour over the chicken, tossing to coat evenly. Cover and refrigerate for 2 hours, turning once.

Place the onion wedges and tomato halves on a baking tray covered with baking paper. Sprinkle with the sugar and drizzle with the balsamic vinegar. Bake for 40 minutes.

Heat a chargrill pan and lightly spray with oil. Remove the chicken from the marinade and cook for 4–5 minutes on each side, or until cooked through. Slice the chicken and serve with the tomato halves, onion wedges and basil.

chicken breast with fruit medley

4 boneless, skinless chicken breasts
80 ml (3 fl oz/⅓ cup) white wine
60 ml (2 fl oz/¼ cup) olive oil
2 teaspoons grated fresh ginger
1 garlic clove, crushed

fruit medley

225 g (8 oz) tinned pineapple slices, drained
1 small mango
2 small kiwi fruit
150 g (5 oz) watermelon, seeds removed
1 tablespoon finely chopped mint leaves

serves 4–6

method Trim the chicken breasts of fat and sinew. Place the chicken in a shallow non-metallic dish. Combine the wine, oil, ginger and garlic in a bowl, and pour over the chicken. Refrigerate, covered, for several hours or overnight, turning occasionally.

To make the fruit medley, finely chop the pineapple, mango, kiwi fruit and watermelon. Combine with the mint and refrigerate.

Preheat a barbecue grill or flat plate to high. Lightly oil the hot barbecue. Cook the chicken for 5–10 minutes each side, or until well browned and cooked through. Serve immediately with the fruit medley.

barbecued garlic chicken

6 garlic cloves, crushed

1½ tablespoons cracked black peppercorns

1 handful chopped coriander (cilantro) leaves
   and stems

4 coriander (cilantro) roots, chopped

80 ml (3 fl oz/⅓ cup) lime juice

1 teaspoon soft brown sugar

1 teaspoon ground turmeric

2 teaspoons light soy sauce

4 boneless, skinless chicken breasts

cucumber and tomato salad

1 Lebanese (short) cucumber, unpeeled

1 large roma (plum) tomato

¼ small red onion, thinly sliced

1 small red chilli, finely chopped

2 tablespoons coriander (cilantro) leaves

2 tablespoons lime juice

1 teaspoon soft brown sugar

1 tablespoon fish sauce

serves 4

method   Blend the garlic, peppercorns, coriander, lime juice, sugar, turmeric and soy sauce in a food processor until smooth, then transfer the marinade to a bowl.

Remove the tenderloins from the chicken breasts. Score the top of each breast three times. Add all the chicken to the marinade, cover and refrigerate for 2 hours or overnight, turning occasionally.

To make the salad, halve the cucumber and scoop out the seeds with a teaspoon. Cut into slices. Halve the tomato lengthways and slice crossways. Combine the cucumber, tomato, onion, chilli and coriander in a small bowl. Drizzle with the combined lime juice, sugar and fish sauce.

Cook the chicken on a lightly greased barbecue grill or flat plate for 3 minutes on each side, until cooked through and tender. Serve the chicken immediately with the salad.

smoked chicken breast

4 boneless, skinless chicken breasts
1 tablespoon olive oil
seasoned pepper, to taste
hickory or mesquite chips, for smoking

serves 4

method Prepare a kettle barbecue for indirect cooking at medium heat. Trim the chicken of excess fat and sinew. Brush the chicken with the oil and sprinkle with the seasoned pepper.

Spoon a pile of hickory or mesquite chips (about 25) over the coals in each charcoal rail.

Cover the barbecue and cook the chicken for 15 minutes. Test with a sharp knife. If the juices do not run clear, cook for another 5–10 minutes, or until cooked through. Serve with chilli noodles.

thai chicken cutlets

12 boneless, skinless chicken thighs
   (1.25 kg/2 lb 12 oz)
6 garlic cloves
1 teaspoon black peppercorns
3 coriander (cilantro) roots and stems,
   roughly chopped

chilli garlic dip

4–5 dried red chillies
2 large garlic cloves, chopped
60 g (2 oz/¼ cup) sugar
80 ml (3 fl oz/⅓ cup) dry cider or rice vinegar
60 ml (2 fl oz/¼ cup) boiling water

serves 4–6

method   Trim the chicken thighs of any excess fat and sinew. Put the garlic, peppercorns, coriander and a pinch of salt salt in a food processor. Process for 20–30 seconds, until the mixture forms a smooth paste. (This can also be done using a mortar and pestle.) Place the chicken in a shallow non-metallic dish. Spread the garlic mixture over the chicken. Refrigerate the chicken, covered, for 1 hour.

To make the chilli garlic dip, soak the chillies in hot water for 20 minutes, then drain and chop finely. Place in a mortar with the garlic and sugar, and grind to a smooth paste. Place the mixture in a small saucepan and add the vinegar, a pinch of salt and boiling water. Bring to the boil, then reduce the heat and simmer for 2–3 minutes. Set aside to cool.

Preheat a barbecue grill or flat plate to high. Grease the hot barbecue and cook the chicken thighs for 5–10 minutes on each side, or until cooked through, turning once. Serve with the chilli garlic dip.

teriyaki chicken wings

8 chicken wings
60 ml (2 fl oz/¼ cup) soy sauce
2 tablespoons dry sherry
2 teaspoons grated fresh ginger
1 garlic clove, crushed
1 tablespoon honey

serves 4

method   Pat the chicken wings dry with paper towels. Trim any excess fat from the wings, and tuck the tips under to form a triangle.

Place the wings in a shallow non-metallic dish. Combine the soy sauce, sherry, ginger, garlic and honey in a bowl, and mix well. Pour the mixture over the chicken wings. Refrigerate, covered, for several hours or overnight. Lightly brush two sheets of aluminium foil with oil. Place 4 wings in a single layer on each piece of foil and wrap completely.

Preheat a barbecue grill or flat plate to high. Cook the parcels on the hot barbecue for about 10 minutes. Remove the parcels from the barbecue and unwrap. Place the wings directly on a lightly greased grill for 3 minutes, or until brown. Turn the wings frequently and brush with any remaining marinade.

chicken fajitas

4 boneless, skinless chicken breasts
2 tablespoons olive oil
60 ml (2 fl oz/¼ cup) lime juice
2 garlic cloves, crushed
1 teaspoon ground cumin
2 tablespoons chopped coriander
    (cilantro) leaves
8 flour tortillas
1 tablespoon olive oil, extra
2 onions, sliced
2 green capsicums (peppers), cut into
    thin strips
125 g (5 oz/1 cup) grated cheddar cheese
1 large avocado, sliced
250 g (9 oz/1 cup) bottled tomato salsa

serves 4

method   Trim the chicken of fat and sinew, and cut into thin strips. Place the chicken in a shallow non-metallic dish. Combine the oil, lime juice, garlic, cumin and coriander in a jug, and mix well. Pour the mixture over the chicken. Cover with plastic wrap, refrigerate for several hours or overnight.

Preheat a barbecue grill or flat plate to high. Wrap the flour tortillas in foil and place on a cool part of the barbecue grill to warm through for 10 minutes. Heat the oil on a flat plate. Cook the onion and capsicum for 5 minutes, or until soft. Move the vegetables to a cooler part of the plate to keep warm.

Place the chicken and marinade on the flat plate and cook for 5 minutes, or until cooked through. Transfer the chicken, vegetables and wrapped tortillas to a serving platter. Make up individual fajitas by placing the chicken, onion and capsicum, cheese and avocado over the tortillas. Top with the salsa and roll up to enclose the filling.

citrus chicken drumsticks

8 chicken drumsticks
80 ml (3 fl oz/⅓ cup) orange juice
80 ml (3 fl oz/⅓ cup) lemon juice
1 teaspoon grated orange zest
1 teaspoon grated lemon zest
1 teaspoon sesame oil
1 tablespoon olive oil
1 spring onion (scallion), finely chopped

serves 4

method Pat the chicken drumsticks dry with paper towels. Trim any excess fat and score the thickest part of the chicken with a knife. Place in a shallow non-metallic dish.

Combine the juices, zests, oils and spring onion. Pour over the chicken and refrigerate, covered, for several hours or overnight, turning occasionally.

Preheat a barbecue grill or flat plate to high. Drain the chicken drumsticks, reserving the marinade. Lightly grease the hot barbecue grill or flat plate. Cook the chicken for 15–20 minutes, or until tender. Brush occasionally with the reserved marinade. Serve immediately.

one-pots

chicken cacciatore

4 tomatoes
1.5 kg (3 lb 5 oz) chicken pieces
20 g (1 oz) butter
1 tablespoon oil
20 g (1 oz) butter, extra
1 large onion, chopped
2 garlic cloves, chopped
1 small green capsicum (pepper), chopped
150 g (5 oz) mushrooms, thickly sliced
1 tablespoon plain (all-purpose) flour
250 ml (9 fl oz/1 cup) dry white wine
1 tablespoon white wine vinegar
2 tablespoons tomato paste
    (concentrated purée)
90 g (3 oz/½ cup) small black olives
4 tablespoons chopped parsley

serves 4

method Score a cross in the base of each tomato. Put the tomatoes in a bowl of boiling water for 30 seconds, then transfer to a bowl of cold water. Drain, peel the skin away from the cross. Halve the tomatoes and remove the seeds. Chop the flesh. Preheat the oven to 180°C (350°F/Gas 4).

Remove excess fat from the chicken pieces and pat dry with paper towels. Heat half the butter and oil in a large flameproof casserole. Cook half the chicken over high heat until browned all over, then set aside. Heat the remaining butter and oil and cook the remaining chicken. Set aside.

Heat the extra butter in the casserole and cook the onion and garlic for 2–3 minutes. Add the capsicum and mushrooms, and cook, stirring, for 3 minutes. Stir in the flour and cook for 1 minute. Add the wine, vinegar, tomato and tomato paste and cook, stirring, for 2 minutes, or until slightly thickened. Return the chicken to the casserole and make sure it is covered by the tomato and onion mixture. Place in the oven and cook, covered, for 1 hour, or until the chicken is tender. Stir in the olives and parsley. Season and serve with pasta.

chicken and lime curry

spice paste

1 large onion, roughly chopped
6 red chillies, seeded and finely chopped
4 garlic cloves, crushed
1 teaspoon finely chopped lemongrass,
white part only
2 teaspoons finely chopped fresh galangal
1 teaspoon ground turmeric

1.6 kg (3 lb 8 oz) chicken
60 ml (2 fl oz/¼ cup) oil
250 ml (9 fl oz/1 cup) coconut milk
2 limes, halved
5 makrut (kaffir lime) leaves, finely shredded
1 tablespoon fish sauce
2 limes, quartered, extra to serve

serves 6

method   To make the spice paste, finely chop all the ingredients in a food processor for a few minutes, or until the mixture is a rough, thick paste.

Cut the chicken through the bone into large bite-sized pieces. Heat the oil in a large heavy-based saucepan or wok and add the spice paste. Cook over low heat, stirring occasionally, for 10 minutes, or until fragrant.

Add the chicken and stir-fry for 2 minutes, making sure the pieces are well covered with the spice paste. Add the coconut milk, 125 ml (4 fl oz/½ cup) water, lime halves and shredded makrut leaves. Simmer for 20–25 minutes, or until the chicken is tender, and cooked through, stirring regularly.

Discard the limes. Add the fish sauce, and serve with the extra lime wedges and steamed rice.

persian chicken

1.5 kg (3 lb 5 oz) chicken thigh cutlets
60 g (2 oz/½ cup) plain (all-purpose) flour
2 tablespoons olive oil
1 large onion, chopped
2 garlic cloves, chopped
½ teaspoon ground cinnamon
4 ripe tomatoes, chopped
6 fresh dates, stones removed, halved
2 tablespoons currants
500 ml (17 fl oz/2 cups) rich chicken stock
2 teaspoons finely grated lemon zest
80 g (3 oz/½ cup) almonds, toasted and
  roughly chopped
2 tablespoons chopped flat-leaf
  (Italian) parsley

serves 6

method Coat the chicken pieces with flour and shake off any excess. Heat the oil in a large heavy-based frying pan over medium heat. Brown the chicken on all sides, turning regularly, and then remove from the pan. Drain any excess oil from the pan.

Add the onion, garlic and ground cinnamon to the pan and cook, stirring regularly, for 5 minutes, until the onion is soft.

Add the tomato, dates, currants and stock, and bring to the boil. Return the chicken to the pan, cover with the sauce, reduce the heat and simmer, uncovered, for 30 minutes. Add the lemon zest and season to taste. Bring back to the boil and boil for 5 minutes, or until thickened. Sprinkle with the almonds and parsley, and serve with buttered rice.

variation *Chicken drumsticks can be used instead of thighs.*

braised chicken with chickpeas

50 g (2 oz) butter
1 onion, roughly chopped
3 garlic cloves, crushed
1 carrot, finely chopped
½ celery stalk, finely chopped
1.5 kg (3 lb 5 oz) chicken pieces
(about 8 portions)
80 ml (3 fl oz/⅓ cup) dry Marsala
250 ml (9 fl oz/1 cup) chicken stock
2 tablespoons lemon juice
40 g (1½ oz/½ cup) fresh breadcrumbs
300 g (11 oz) tinned chickpeas, drained
and rinsed
200 g (7 oz) button mushrooms, sliced
2 tablespoons shredded mint
2 tablespoons chopped flat-leaf
(Italian) parsley

serves 4

method   Heat half the butter in a large, heavy-based saucepan and cook the onion over medium heat until soft and golden. Add the garlic, carrot and celery and cook over gentle heat for 5 minutes. Remove from the pan and set aside.

Melt the remaining butter in the pan and brown the chicken in batches over high heat. Return all the chicken to the pan with the carrot and celery mixture. Quickly add the Marsala and stir well, scraping the sides and base of the pan. Add the stock and lemon juice, and bring to the boil. Reduce the heat and simmer gently for 1 hour, stirring occasionally.

Remove the chicken and keep warm. In a food processor, purée the contents of the pan, then add the breadcrumbs and blend for another 15 seconds.

Return the chicken to the pan, pour in the purée, add the chickpeas and mushrooms and simmer, covered, for 15 minutes. Season to taste, and scatter with mint and parsley to serve.

chicken and peanut panang curry

1 tablespoon oil
1 large red onion, chopped
1–2 tablespoons panang curry paste
250 ml (9 fl oz/1 cup) coconut milk
500 g (1 lb 2 oz) boneless, skinless chicken
   thighs, cut into bite-sized pieces
4 makrut (kaffir lime) leaves
60 g (2 oz/¼ cup) coconut cream
1 tablespoon fish sauce
1 tablespoon lime juice
2 teaspoons soft brown sugar
80 g (3 oz/½ cup) roasted peanuts, chopped
1 handful Thai basil
80 g (3 oz/½ cup) chopped fresh pineapple
chilli sauce, to serve

serves 4

method Heat the oil in a wok or large frying pan. Add the onion and curry paste to the wok and stir over medium heat for 2 minutes. Add the coconut milk and bring to the boil.

Add the chicken and makrut leaves to the wok, then reduce the heat and cook for 15 minutes. Remove the chicken with a wire mesh strainer or slotted spoon. Simmer the sauce for 5 minutes, or until it is reduced and quite thick.

Return the chicken to the wok. Add the coconut cream, fish sauce, lime juice and brown sugar. Cook for 5 minutes. Stir in the peanuts, basil and pineapple. Serve with steamed rice.

chicken and mushroom casserole

20 g (1 oz) dried porcini mushrooms
30 g (1 oz/¼ cup) plain (all-purpose) flour
1.5 kg (3 lb 5 oz) chicken pieces
2 tablespoons oil
1 large onion, chopped
2 garlic cloves, crushed
60 ml (2 fl oz/¼ cup) chicken stock
80 ml (3 fl oz/⅓ cup) dry white wine
425 g (15 oz) tinned peeled whole tomatoes
1 tablespoon balsamic vinegar
3 thyme sprigs
1 bay leaf
300 g (11 oz) field mushrooms,
thickly sliced

serves 4

method   Preheat the oven to 180°C (350°F/Gas 4). Put the porcini mushrooms in a bowl and cover with 60 ml (2 fl oz/¼ cup) boiling water. Leave for 5 minutes, or until the mushrooms are rehydrated.

Season the flour with salt and freshly ground pepper. Lightly toss the chicken in the flour to coat and shake off any excess.

Heat the oil in a flameproof casserole and cook the chicken in batches until well browned all over. Set aside. Add the onion and garlic to the casserole and cook for 3–5 minutes, or until the onion softens. Stir in the stock.

Return the chicken to the casserole with the porcini mushrooms and any remaining liquid, white wine, tomatoes, vinegar, thyme and bay leaf. Cover and cook in the oven for 30 minutes.

After 30 minutes, remove the lid and add the field mushrooms. Return to the oven and cook, uncovered, for 15–20 minutes, or until the sauce thickens slightly. Serve with boiled potatoes sprinkled with parsley.

chicken mole

8 chicken drumsticks
plain (all-purpose) flour, for dusting
cooking oil spray
1 large onion, finely chopped
2 garlic cloves, finely chopped
1 teaspoon ground cumin
1 teaspoon chilli powder
2 teaspoons cocoa powder
440 g (15 oz) tinned tomatoes,
    roughly chopped
440 g (15 oz) tomato paste
    (concentrated purée)
250 ml (9 fl oz/1 cup) chicken stock
toasted slivered almonds, to garnish
chopped parsley, to garnish

serves 4

method Remove and discard the chicken skin. Wipe the chicken with paper towels and lightly dust with the flour. Spray a large, deep, non-stick frying pan with oil. Cook the chicken for 8 minutes over high heat, turning until golden brown. Remove and set aside.

Add the onion, garlic, cumin, chilli powder, cocoa, 1 teaspoon salt, $1/2$ teaspoon black pepper and 60 ml (2 fl oz/$1/4$ cup) water to the pan and cook for 5 minutes, or until softened.

Stir in the tomato, tomato paste and chicken stock. Bring to the boil, then add the chicken drumsticks, cover and simmer for 45 minutes, or until tender. Uncover and simmer for 5 minutes, until the mixture is thick. Garnish with the almonds and parsley.

note *This is a traditional Mexican dish, usually flavoured with a special type of dark chocolate rather than cocoa powder.*

spicy garlic chicken

1.4 kg (3 lb 2 oz) chicken
1 handful coriander (cilantro) leaves with roots
2 tablespoons olive oil
4 garlic cloves, crushed
2 red onions, thinly sliced
1 large red capsicum (pepper), cut into squares
1 teaspoon ground ginger
1 teaspoon chilli powder
1 teaspoon caraway seeds, crushed
1 teaspoon ground turmeric
2 teaspoons ground coriander
2 teaspoons ground cumin
60 g (2 oz/½ cup) raisins
90 g (3 oz/½ cup) black olives
1 teaspoon finely grated lemon zest

serves 4–6

method   Trim the chicken of excess fat and sinew. Cut the chicken into 12 serving pieces. Finely chop the coriander roots, reserving the leaves.

Heat the oil in a large heavy-based frying pan. Add the garlic, onion, capsicum, ginger, chilli powder, caraway seeds, turmeric, coriander, cumin and coriander roots. Cook over medium heat for 10 minutes.

Add the chicken pieces and stir until combined. Add 375 ml (13 fl oz/1½ cups) water and bring to the boil. Reduce the heat and simmer for 45 minutes, or until the chicken is tender and cooked through.

Add the raisins, black olives and lemon zest and simmer for a further 5 minutes. Serve with bread and green vegetables. May be served sprinkled with the reserved coriander leaves.

variation   *Chicken pieces may be used instead of a whole chicken.*

chicken and orange casserole

2 small chickens
1 tablespoon olive oil
2 thick bacon slices, rind removed and
   thinly sliced
50 g (2 oz) butter
16 baby onions, peeled, ends left intact
2–3 garlic cloves, crushed
3 teaspoons grated fresh ginger
2 teaspoons grated orange zest
2 teaspoons ground cumin
2 teaspoons ground coriander
2 tablespoons honey
250 ml (9 fl oz/1 cup) fresh orange juice
250 ml (9 fl oz/1 cup) dry white wine
125 ml (4 fl oz/½ cup) chicken or
   vegetable stock
350 g (12 oz) baby carrots
1 large parsnip, peeled

serves 4–6

method   Using a pair of kitchen scissors, cut each chicken into 8 pieces, discarding the backbone. Remove any excess fat and discard (remove the skin as well, if preferred).

Heat about a teaspoon of the oil in a large, deep, heavy-based saucepan. Add the bacon and cook over medium heat for 2–3 minutes or until just crisp. Remove from the pan and drain on paper towels. Add the remaining oil and half the butter to the pan. Cook the onions, stirring occasionally, until dark golden brown. Remove from the pan and set aside. Add the chicken pieces to the pan and brown in batches over medium heat. Remove from the pan, drain on paper towels.

Add the remaining butter to the pan. Stir in the garlic, ginger, orange zest, cumin, coriander and honey, and cook, stirring, for 1 minute. Add the orange juice, wine and stock to the pan. Bring to the boil, then reduce the heat and simmer for 1 minute. Return the chicken pieces to the pan, cover and simmer over low heat for 40 minutes. Return the onions and bacon to the pan and simmer, covered, for 15 minutes. Remove the lid and leave to simmer for a further 15 minutes.

Trim the carrots, leaving a little stalk, and wash well or peel, if necessary. Cut the parsnip into small batons. Add the carrots and parsnip to the pan. Cover and cook for 5–10 minutes, or until the carrots and parsnip are just tender. To serve, put 2–3 chicken pieces on each plate, arrange the vegetables around it and spoon a little sauce over the top.

spicy chicken and beans

1 tablespoon olive oil
4 spring onions (scallions), finely chopped
1 celery stalk, finely chopped
1 jalapeño chilli, seeded and chopped
500 g (1 lb 2 oz) minced (ground) chicken
3 garlic cloves, crushed
¼ teaspoon ground cinnamon
¼ teaspoon chilli powder
1 teaspoon ground cumin
2 teaspoons plain (all-purpose) flour
425 g (15 oz) tinned chopped tomatoes
125 ml (4 fl oz/½ cup) chicken stock
2 x 300 g (11 oz) tinned butter
beans, drained
2 teaspoons soft brown sugar
4 tablespoons finely chopped coriander
(cilantro) leaves

serves 4

method   Heat the oil in a large frying pan, add the spring onion and cook until softened. Add the celery and chilli and cook for 1–2 minutes. Increase the heat, add the mince and brown, breaking up lumps with a fork or wooden spoon. Stir in the garlic, cinnamon, chilli powder and cumin. Cook for 1 minute. Add the flour to the pan and stir well.

Stir in the tomato and stock. Bring the mixture to the boil, reduce the heat and simmer, covered, for 10–15 minutes.

Add the butter beans to the pan and simmer for another 15 minutes, until the liquid is reduced to a thick sauce. Add the sugar and season, to taste. Just before serving, scatter the coriander over the top.

coq au vin

2 thyme sprigs
4 parsley sprigs
2 bay leaves
2 kg (4 lb 8 oz) chicken pieces
seasoned plain (all-purpose) flour
60 ml (2 fl oz/¼ cup) oil
4 thick bacon slices, sliced
12 baby onions
2 garlic cloves, crushed
2 tablespoons brandy
375 ml (13 fl oz/1½ cups) dry red wine
375 ml (13 fl oz/1½ cups) chicken stock
60 g (2 oz/¼ cup) tomato paste
   (concentrated purée)
250 g (9 oz) button mushrooms

serves 6

method   Make a bouquet garni by wrapping the thyme, parsley and bay leaves in a small square of muslin and tying them well with string, or tying them between two 5 cm (2 inch) lengths of celery.

Toss the chicken in the seasoned flour to coat, shaking off any excess. In a heavy-based saucepan, heat 2 tablespoons of the oil and brown the chicken in batches over medium heat. Drain on paper towels.

Wipe the pan clean with paper towels and heat the remaining oil. Add the bacon, onions and garlic and cook, stirring, until the onions are browned. Add the chicken, brandy, red wine, chicken stock, bouquet garni and tomato paste. Bring to the boil, reduce the heat and simmer, covered, for 30 minutes.

Stir in the mushrooms and simmer, uncovered, for 10 minutes, or until the chicken is tender and the sauce has thickened. Remove the bouquet garni.

note   *Don't be tempted to use poor-quality wine for cooking, as the taste will affect the flavour of the dish.*

vietnamese chicken curry

1.5 kg (3 lb 5 oz) chicken pieces, such as thighs,
drumsticks and wings
2 tablespoons oil
4 garlic cloves, finely chopped
5 cm (2 inch) piece ginger, finely chopped
2 lemongrass stems, white part only,
finely chopped
2 teaspoons dried chilli flakes
2 tablespoons Asian curry powder
(see Note)
2 brown onions, chopped
2 teaspoons sugar
375 ml (13 fl oz/1½ cups) coconut milk
snipped garlic chives, to serve
coriander (cilantro) leaves, to serve
roasted peanuts, to serve

serves 4

method Using a large heavy knife or cleaver, chop each piece of chicken into two, chopping straight through the bone. Pat the chicken pieces dry with paper towels.

Heat the oil in a large deep frying pan. Add the garlic, ginger, lemongrass, chilli and curry powder and stir constantly over medium heat for 3 minutes, or until fragrant. Add the chicken pieces, onion, sugar and 1 teaspoon of salt; toss gently. Cover, cook for 8 minutes, or until the onion has softened and then toss well to coat the chicken evenly with the curry mixture. Cover again and cook for 15 minutes over low heat—the chicken will gently braise, producing its own liquid.

Add the coconut milk and water to the pan. Bring to the boil, stirring occasionally. Reduce the heat and simmer, uncovered, for 30 minutes, or until the chicken is very tender. Serve garnished with the chives, coriander and peanuts.

note *Asian curry powders are available from speciality shops. There are different mixtures available for meat, chicken or fish.*

creamy tomato and chicken stew

4 bacon slices
2 tablespoons oil
50 g (2 oz) butter
300 g (11 oz) small button mushrooms,
  halved
1.5 kg (3 lb 5 oz) chicken pieces
2 onions, chopped
2 garlic cloves, crushed
400 g (14 oz) tinned whole peeled
  tomatoes
250 ml (9 fl oz/1 cup) chicken stock
250 ml (9 fl oz/1 cup) cream
2 tablespoons chopped flat-leaf
  (Italian) parsley
2 tablespoons lemon thyme leaves

serves 4–6

method Chop the bacon into large pieces. Place a large, heavy-based saucepan over medium heat. Brown the bacon, then remove and set aside on paper towels.

Heat half the oil and a third of the butter in the pan until foaming, then stir in the mushrooms and cook until softened and golden brown. Remove from the saucepan with a slotted spoon.

Add the remaining oil to the pan with a little more butter. When the oil is hot, brown the chicken pieces in batches over high heat until the skin is golden all over and a little crisp. Remove from the pan.

Heat the remaining butter in the pan. Add the onion and garlic and cook over medium–high heat for about 3 minutes, or until softened. Pour in the tomato, stock and cream. Return the bacon, mushrooms and chicken to the pan and simmer over medium–low heat for 25 minutes. Stir in the herbs, season with salt and freshly ground pepper and simmer for another 5 minutes before serving.

chicken and spinach curry

2 tablespoons ghee (clarified butter)
1 kg (2 lb 4 oz) chicken drumsticks and thighs
1 tablespoon hot curry powder
1 tablespoon curry paste
½ teaspoon black mustard seeds
½ teaspoon ground coriander
1 teaspoon paprika
¼ teaspoon cinnamon
½ teaspoon cumin
½ teaspoon turmeric
1 tablespoon finely chopped coriander
(cilantro) root
2 garlic cloves, crushed
2 cm (¾ inch) piece ginger, grated
1 onion, chopped
1 kg (2 lb 4 oz) potatoes, quartered
375 ml (13 fl oz/1½ cups) chicken stock
1 tablespoon lemon juice
2 x 425 g (15 oz) tinned peeled
whole tomatoes
250 g (9 oz) packet frozen spinach, defrosted
60 ml (2 fl oz/¼ cup) coconut cream

serves 4

method Melt 1 tablespoon of ghee in a heavy-based saucepan, and cook the chicken in batches for 2–3 minutes, or until browned all over. Remove from the pan. Melt the remaining ghee in the same pan, add the curry powder, paste and remaining dry spices, and cook over low heat for 1–2 minutes, or until fragrant. Increase the heat, add the coriander root, garlic, ginger and chopped onion, and cook for 3–5 minutes, or until the onion is soft.

Return the chicken pieces to the pan, add the potato and gently toss in the spices. Season generously with salt and pepper. Pour in the chicken stock, and stir to ensure that any spices on the bottom of the pan are incorporated. Add the lemon juice and tomatoes, bring to the boil, then reduce the heat and simmer for 1–1½ hours, or until the potato is tender and the chicken meat is falling off the bones.

Carefully remove the chicken from the pan, let it cool slightly and pull the meat off the bones. Return to the pan. Stir in the spinach and coconut cream and cook for 3–5 minutes, or until heated through. Serve with rice.

creamy chicken with mushrooms

2 tablespoons olive oil

200 g (7 oz) button mushrooms, halved

200 g (7 oz) field mushrooms, chopped

1 small red capsicum (pepper), sliced

4 boneless, skinless chicken breasts, cut into bite-sized pieces

2 tablespoons plain (all-purpose) flour

250 ml (9 fl oz/1 cup) chicken stock

125 ml (4 fl oz/½ cup) red wine

3 spring onions (scallions), finely chopped

310 ml (11 fl oz/1¼ cups) cream

1 tablespoon chopped chives

1 tablespoon chopped flat-leaf (Italian) parsley, extra, to garnish

¼ teaspoon turmeric

serves 6

method Heat the oil in a large heavy-based saucepan and add the button and field mushrooms and capsicum. Cook over medium heat for 4 minutes, or until soft. Remove and set aside.

Add the chicken to the pan in batches and brown quickly over medium–high heat. Sprinkle with the flour and cook for a further 2 minutes, or until the flour is golden. Add the stock and wine and bring to the boil. Cover and simmer for 10 minutes, or until the chicken is tender.

Add the spring onion and cream, return to the boil and simmer for 10–15 minutes, until the cream has reduced and thickened. Return the mushrooms and capsicum to the pan and add the chives, parsley and turmeric. Stir, season to taste and simmer for a further 5 minutes to heat through. Sprinkle with chopped parsley, just before serving.

chicken paprika

800 g (1 lb 12 oz) boneless, skinless
chicken thighs
60 g (2 oz/½ cup) plain (all-purpose) flour
2 tablespoons oil
2 onions, chopped
1–2 garlic cloves, crushed
2 tablespoons sweet paprika
125 ml (4 fl oz/½ cup) good-quality dry
red wine
1 tablespoon tomato paste
(concentrated purée)
425 g (15 oz) tinned chopped tomatoes
200 g (7 oz) button mushrooms
125 ml (4 fl oz/½ cup) chicken stock
80 g (3 oz/⅓ cup) sour cream

serves 4–6

method   Rinse the chicken and dry well with paper towel. Trim the chicken of excess fat and sinew. Cut the chicken into 3 cm (1¼ inch) pieces. Season the flour with salt and pepper. Toss the chicken in the seasoned flour, shake off the excess and reserve the flour. Heat half the oil in a large heavy-based frying pan. Cook the chicken pieces quickly in batches over medium–high heat. Remove from the pan and drain on paper towels.

Heat the remaining oil in the pan and add the onion and garlic. Cook, stirring, until the onion is soft. Add the paprika and reserved flour, and stir for 1 minute. Add the chicken, red wine, tomato paste and undrained crushed tomato. Bring to the boil, then reduce the heat and simmer, covered, for 15 minutes.

Add the mushrooms and chicken stock. Simmer, covered, for a further 10 minutes. Add the sour cream and stir until heated through, but do not allow to boil.

green chicken curry

1 tablespoon oil
1 onion, chopped
1–2 tablespoons green curry paste
375 ml (13 fl oz/1½ cups) coconut milk
500 g (1 lb 2 oz) boneless, skinless chicken
  thighs, cut into bite-sized pieces
100 g (4 oz) green beans, cut into
  short pieces
6 makrut (kaffir lime) leaves
1 tablespoon fish sauce
1 tablespoon lime juice
1 teaspoon finely grated lime zest
2 teaspoons soft brown sugar
1 handful coriander (cilantro) leaves

serves 4

method   Heat the oil in a wok or a heavy-based frying pan. Add the onion and curry paste to the wok and cook for about 1 minute, stirring constantly. Add the coconut milk and 125 ml (4 fl oz/½ cup) water and bring to the boil.

Add the chicken pieces, beans and makrut leaves to the wok, and stir to combine. Simmer, uncovered, for 15–20 minutes, or until the chicken is tender. Add the fish sauce, lime juice, lime zest and brown sugar to the wok, and stir to combine. Sprinkle with fresh coriander leaves just before serving. Serve with steamed rice.

note   *Chicken thighs are sweet in flavour and a very good texture for curries. You can use chicken breasts instead, if you prefer. Do not overcook them or they will be tough.*

apricot chicken

6 chicken thigh cutlets
425 ml (15 fl oz) apricot nectar
40 g (1½ oz) packet French onion soup mix
425 g (15 oz) tinned apricot halves in natural juice, drained
60 g (2 oz/¼ cup) sour cream

serves 6

method   Preheat the oven to 180°C (350°F/Gas 4). Remove the skin from the chicken thigh cutlets. Put the chicken in an ovenproof dish. Mix the apricot nectar with the French onion soup mix until well combined, and pour over the chicken.

Bake, covered, for 50 minutes, then add the apricot halves and bake for a further 5 minutes. Stir in the sour cream just before serving. Delicious with creamy mashed potato or rice to soak up the juices.

note   *If you are looking for a healthy alternative, use low-fat sour cream in place of the full-fat version.*

pies and roasts

creamy chicken, sage and tarragon pie

1.5 kg (3 lb 5 oz) boneless, skinless
   chicken thighs
2 tablespoons olive oil
2 bacon slices, finely chopped
1 onion, roughly chopped
4 sage leaves, chopped
1 tablespoon chopped tarragon
45 g (1½ oz) butter, melted
2 tablespoons plain (all-purpose) flour
125 ml (4 fl oz/½ cup) milk
225 g (8 oz) tinned creamed corn
2 sheets ready-rolled puff pastry
1 egg, lightly beaten

serves 4–6

method   Preheat the oven to 210°C (415°F/Gas 6–7). Brush a 23 cm (9 inch) pie dish with butter. Cut the chicken into bite-sized pieces. Heat the oil in a large frying pan. Add the chicken, bacon and onion, and cook over medium heat for 5 minutes, or until browned. Add the sage, tarragon, 250 ml (9 fl oz/1 cup) water, salt and freshly ground pepper. Bring to the boil, reduce the heat and simmer, covered, for 25 minutes, or until the chicken is cooked through. Drain, reserving the juices.

Melt the butter in a heavy-based frying pan. Add the flour and stir over low heat for 1 minute. Remove from the heat and gradually add the milk and reserved juice, stirring until smooth. Stir over medium heat until thickened. Stir in the chicken mixture and corn. Spoon into the pie dish.

Brush a sheet of pastry with egg and top with a second sheet. Brush the rim of the pie dish with egg and place the pastry over the filling. Trim any excess. Decorate the pie with pastry. Brush with egg and make a few slits in the top. Bake for 15 minutes, then reduce the heat to 180°C (350°F/Gas 4) and bake for 10–15 minutes, or until crisp and golden. Allow to slightly cool for 5 minutes before cutting.

spring chicken with honey glaze

2 small (1.5 kg/3 lb 5 oz) chickens
1 tablespoon light olive oil

honey glaze

90 g (3 oz/¼ cup) honey
juice and finely grated zest of 1 lemon
1 tablespoon finely chopped rosemary
1 tablespoon dry white wine
1 tablespoon white wine vinegar
2 teaspoons dijon mustard
1½ tablespoons olive oil

serves 6–8

method   Preheat the oven to 180°C (350°F/Gas 4). Halve the chickens by cutting down either side of the backbone. Discard the backbones. Cut the chickens into quarters, then brush with the oil and season lightly. Place on a rack in a roasting tin, skin side down, and roast for 20 minutes.

To make the honey glaze, combine the honey, lemon juice, zest, rosemary, wine, vinegar, mustard and oil in a small saucepan. Bring to the boil, then reduce the heat and simmer for about 5 minutes.

After cooking one side, turn the chickens over and baste well with the warm glaze. Return to the oven and roast for 20 minutes. Baste once more and cook for a further 15 minutes.

chicken and leek cobbler

50 g (2 oz) butter
1 kg (2 lb 4 oz) boneless, skinless chicken
   breasts, cut into thick strips
1 large (225 g/8 oz) leek, trimmed and
   thinly sliced
1 celery stalk, thinly sliced
1 tablespoon plain (all-purpose) flour
250 ml (9 fl oz/1 cup) chicken stock
250 ml (9 fl oz/1 cup) cream
3 teaspoons dijon mustard
3 teaspoons drained and rinsed green
   peppercorns

topping

400 g (14 oz) potatoes, quartered
165 g (6 oz/1⅓ cups) self-raising flour
½ teaspoon salt
30 g (1 oz/¼ cup) grated mature cheddar
   cheese
100 g (4 oz) cold butter, chopped
1 egg yolk, lightly beaten, to glaze
1 tablespoon milk, to glaze

serves 4–6

method   Melt half the butter in a pan. When it begins to foam, add the chicken and cook until golden. Remove from the pan. Add the remaining butter and cook the leek and celery over medium heat until soft. Return the chicken to the pan.

Sprinkle the flour over the chicken and stir for about 1 minute. Remove from the heat and stir in the stock and cream. Mix well, making sure that there are no lumps. Return to the heat. Bring to the boil, then reduce the heat and simmer for about 20 minutes. Add the mustard, and peppercorns and season. Transfer the mixture to a 1.25–1.5 litre (5–6 cup) capacity casserole dish and allow to cool. Preheat the oven to 200°C (400°F/Gas 6).

To make the topping, cook the potato in a saucepan of boiling water until tender. Drain and mash until smooth. Put the flour and salt in a food processor and add the cheese and butter. Process in short bursts until the mixture forms crumbs. Add to the mashed potato and bring together to form a dough.

Roll out the dough on a lightly floured surface, until it is 1 cm (½ inch) thick. Cut into circles with a 6 cm (2½ inch) diameter pastry cutter. Keep re-rolling the pastry scraps until all the dough is used. Arrange circles on top of the cooled chicken and leek filling.

Brush the dough with the combined egg yolk and milk. Bake for 30 minutes, or until heated through and the pastry is golden.

chicken with baked eggplant and tomato

1 red capsicum (pepper)
1 eggplant (aubergine)
3 tomatoes, cut into quarters
200 g (7 oz) large button mushrooms, halved
1 onion, cut into thin wedges
cooking oil spray
1½ tablespoons tomato paste
(concentrated purée)
125 ml (4 fl oz/½ cup) chicken stock
60 ml (2 fl oz/¼ cup) white wine
2 lean bacon slices
4 boneless, skinless chicken breasts
4 small rosemary sprigs

serves 4

method   Preheat the oven to 200°C (400°F/Gas 6). Cut the capsicum and eggplant into bite-sized pieces and combine with the tomato, mushrooms and onion in a baking dish. Spray with oil and bake for 1 hour, or until starting to brown and soften, stirring once.

Pour the combined tomato paste, stock and wine into the dish and bake for 10 minutes, until thickened.

Meanwhile, discard the fat and rind from the bacon and cut in half. Wrap a strip of bacon around each chicken breast and secure it underneath with a toothpick. Poke a sprig of fresh rosemary underneath the bacon. Pan-fry in a lightly oiled, non-stick frying pan over medium heat until golden on both sides. Cover and cook for 10–15 minutes, or until the chicken is tender and cooked. Remove the toothpicks. Serve the chicken on the vegetable mixture, surrounded with the sauce.

chicken and sugar snap pea parcels

200 g (7 oz) sugar snap peas
1 tablespoon vegetable oil
6 boneless, skinless chicken thighs, cut into
 1 cm (½ inch) thick strips
40 g (1½ oz) butter
2 tablespoons plain (all-purpose) flour
185 ml (6 fl oz/¾ cup) chicken stock
170 ml (6 fl oz/⅔ cup) dry white wine
1 tablespoon wholegrain mustard
150 g (5 oz) feta cheese, cut into 1 cm
 (½ inch) cubes
50 g (2 oz/⅓ cup) sliced sun-dried tomatoes,
 finely chopped
24 sheets filo pastry
60 g (2 oz) butter, extra, melted
sesame seeds, to garnish
sunflower seeds, to garnish

serves 8

method Preheat the oven to 210°C (415°F/Gas 6–7). Top and tail the sugar snap peas, then plunge into boiling water for 1 minute, or until bright in colour but still crunchy. Drain well.

Heat the oil in a heavy-based frying pan. Cook the chicken quickly, in small batches, over medium heat until well browned. Remove and drain on paper towels.

Melt the butter in a saucepan and add the flour. Stir over low heat for 2 minutes, until the flour mixture is light golden and bubbling. Add the stock, wine and mustard, stirring until the mixture is smooth. Stir constantly over medium heat until the mixture boils and thickens. Stir in the chicken, sugar snap peas, feta and tomato and mix gently. Remove from the heat and allow to cool. Divide the mixture evenly into eight portions.

Brush three sheets of the pastry with melted butter. Place the sheets on top of each other. Place one portion of the mixture at one short end of the pastry. Roll and fold the pastry, enclosing the filling to form a parcel. Brush with more butter and place seam side down on a greased baking tray. Repeat with the remaining pastry, butter and filling. Brush the tops with butter. Sprinkle with the sesame seeds and sunflower seeds. Bake for 20 minutes, or until golden brown and cooked through. Serve with a mixed green leaf salad.

chicken and bacon gougère

60 g (2 oz) butter
1–2 garlic cloves, crushed
1 red onion, chopped
3 bacon slices, chopped
30 g (1 oz/¼ cup) plain (all-purpose) flour
375 ml (13 fl oz/1½ cups) milk
125 ml (4 fl oz/½ cup) cream
2 teaspoons wholegrain mustard
250 g (9 oz) cooked chicken, chopped
1 handful chopped parsley
1 tablespoon grated parmesan cheese

choux pastry

60 g (2 oz) butter, chopped
60 g (2 oz/½ cup) plain (all-purpose) flour
2 eggs, lightly beaten
35 g (1 oz/⅓ cup) grated parmesan cheese

serves 6

method Melt the butter in a frying pan and cook the garlic, onion and bacon for 5–7 minutes, stirring occasionally, until soft but not browned. Stir in the flour and cook for 1 minute. Gradually add the milk and stir until thickened. Simmer for 2 minutes, then add the cream and wholegrain mustard. Remove from the heat and fold in the chopped chicken and parsley. Season with pepper.

To make the pastry, place the butter and 125 ml (4 fl oz/½ cup) water in a saucepan and stir until melted. Bring to the boil. Add the flour and beat for 2 minutes, or until the mixture leaves the side of the pan. Cool for 5 minutes. Gradually mix in the egg with an electric beater, until thick and glossy. Add the parmesan cheese.

Preheat the oven to 210°C (415°F/Gas 6–7). Grease a deep 23 cm (9 inch) ovenproof dish, pour in the filling and spoon heaped tablespoons of choux pastry around the outside. Bake for 10 minutes, then reduce the oven to 180°C (350°F/Gas 4) and bake for 20 minutes, or until the pastry is puffed and golden. Sprinkle with parmesan cheese.

chicken pot pies with herb scones

60 g (2 oz) butter, melted, plus extra for greasing
1 onion, chopped
40 g (1½ oz/⅓ cup) plain (all-purpose) flour
670 ml (23 fl oz/2⅔ cups) milk
125 g (5 oz/1 cup) grated cheddar cheese
2 teaspoons wholegrain mustard
450 g (1 lb/2½ cups) chopped cooked chicken
200 g (7 oz/2 cups) frozen mixed vegetables

topping

250 g (9 oz/2 cups) self-raising flour
15 g (½ oz) butter
250 ml (9 fl oz/1 cup) milk
2 tablespoons chopped parsley
1 tablespoon milk, extra

serves 6

method Preheat the oven to 210°C (415°F/Gas 6–7). Grease six 250 ml (9 fl oz/1 cup) ovenproof dishes with butter. Heat the butter in a large heavy-based frying pan over medium heat. Add the onion and cook until soft. Add the flour and stir for 1 minute, or until lightly golden and bubbling. Gradually add the milk, stirring constantly, until the sauce boils and thickens. Remove from the heat. Stir in the cheddar, mustard, chicken and vegetables. Spoon the mixture evenly into the prepared dishes.

To make the topping, place the flour in a bowl. Using your fingertips, rub the butter into the flour, until the mixture is crumbly. Make a well in the centre. Stir in the milk and parsley with a flat-bladed knife. Using a cutting action, stir until the mixture is soft and sticky.

On a floured surface, gather the dough into a ball and roll to 2.5 cm (1 inch) thick. Cut into rounds with a 4.5 cm (1¾ inch) cutter. Re-roll the pastry scraps to cut more rounds. Place three rounds on top of each chicken pot. Brush the tops with milk. Bake for 25 minutes, until the scones are cooked and the pies heated through.

moroccan chicken filo pie

1 tablespoon olive oil
1 red onion, chopped
2–3 garlic cloves, crushed
2 teaspoons grated fresh ginger
1 teaspoon ground turmeric
1 teaspoon ground cumin
1 teaspoon ground coriander
500 g (1 lb 2 oz) cooked chicken, shredded
60 g (2 oz/½ cup) slivered almonds, toasted
1 handful chopped coriander (cilantro) leaves
4 tablespoons chopped parsley
1 teaspoon grated lemon zest
2 tablespoons chicken stock or water
1 egg, lightly beaten
9 sheets filo pastry
50 g (2 oz) butter, melted
1 teaspoon caster (superfine) sugar
¼ teaspoon ground cinnamon

serves 4–6

method   Heat the oil in a frying pan and cook the onion, garlic and ginger, stirring, for 5 minutes, or until the onion is just soft. Stir in the ground turmeric, cumin and coriander and cook, stirring, for 1–2 minutes. Remove from the heat and stir in the shredded chicken, almonds, coriander, parsley and lemon zest. Leave to cool for 5 minutes, then stir in the stock or water and the beaten egg.

Preheat the oven to 180°C (350°F/Gas 4). Grease a baking tray. Cut 6 sheets of filo pastry into 30 cm (12 inch) squares, retaining the extra strips. Cut each of the remaining sheets into 3 equal strips. Cover with a damp tea towel. Brush 1 square with the butter and place on the baking tray. Lay another square at an angle on top and brush with the butter. Repeat with the other squares to form a rough 8-pointed star. Spoon the chicken mixture into the centre, leaving a 5 cm (2 inch) border. Turn the pastry edge in, leaving the centre open. Brush the pastry strips with the butter and lightly scrunch, lay them over the top of the pie. Sprinkle with the sugar and cinnamon. Bake for 25 minutes.

spicy spatchcocked chicken

2 small chickens (750 g/1 lb 10 oz each) or
   1 kg (2 lb 4 oz) chicken drumsticks
2 tablespoons malt vinegar or lemon juice
1½ teaspoons chilli powder
1½ teaspoons ground sweet paprika
2 teaspoons ground coriander
2 teaspoons ground cumin
1 teaspoon garam masala
1 tablespoon finely grated fresh ginger
1 tablespoon crushed garlic
80 g (3 oz/⅓ cup) plain yoghurt
60 ml (2 fl oz/¼ cup) ghee, melted, or oil

serves 4

method Pat the chickens dry with paper towels. Combine the vinegar, chilli, paprika, coriander, cumin, garam masala, ginger, garlic, salt and yoghurt in a large non-metallic bowl.

Using scissors, remove the backbones from the chickens. Turn the chickens over and flatten. Make several slashes in the skin. Place the chickens on a tray and coat well with the marinade, working it well into the flesh. Cover and refrigerate for 4 hours.

Place the chickens on a cold, lightly oiled grill. Brush with the melted ghee. Cook the chickens under a moderately hot grill for 20 minutes, or until cooked through, turning halfway through cooking and brushing occasionally with any remaining marinade. Serve the chickens with breads such as naan or chapatis, and lemon wedges.

note *If you remove the chicken skin, the flavours of the marinade spices are able to penetrate the flesh much more effectively. Also, the finished dish will contain far less fat than if the skin were left on.*

mustard chicken and asparagus quiche

250 g (9 oz/2 cups) plain (all-purpose) flour
100 g (4 oz) cold butter, chopped
1 egg yolk

filling

150 g (5 oz) asparagus, chopped
25 g (1 oz) butter
1 onion, chopped
60 g (2 oz/¼ cup) wholegrain mustard
200 g (7 oz) soft cream cheese
125 ml (4 fl oz/½ cup) cream
3 eggs, lightly beaten
200 g (7 oz) cooked chicken, chopped

serves 8

method   Process the flour and butter until crumbly. Add the egg yolk and 60 ml (2 fl oz/¼ cup) of water. Process in short bursts until the mixture comes together. Add a little extra water if needed. Gather dough into a ball on a floured surface. Cover with plastic wrap and chill for 30 minutes. Grease a 19 cm (7½ inch) diameter deep loose-based flan tin.

Roll out the pastry and line the tin. Trim off any excess. Place the tin on a baking tray and refrigerate for 10 minutes. Preheat the oven to 200°C (400°F/Gas 6). Cover the pastry with baking paper and fill evenly with baking beads. Bake for 10 minutes. Remove the paper and beads and bake for about 10 minutes, or until the pastry is lightly browned and dry. Cool. Reduce the oven to 180°C (350°F/Gas 4).

To make the filling, steam the asparagus until tender. Drain and pat dry. Melt the butter in a saucepan over low heat and cook the onion until soft. Remove from the heat and add the mustard and cream cheese, stirring until the cheese has melted. Cool. Add the cream, eggs, chicken and asparagus and mix well. Spoon the filling into the pastry shell and season. Bake for 50 minutes to 1 hour, or until puffed and set. Cool for 15 minutes before cutting.

roast chicken with breadcrumb stuffing

3 bacon slices, finely chopped
6 slices wholegrain bread, crusts removed
3 spring onions (scallions), chopped
2 tablespoons chopped pecans
2 teaspoons currants
1 handful finely chopped flat-leaf (Italian)
   parsley
1 egg, lightly beaten
60 ml (2 fl oz/¼ cup) milk
1.4 kg (3 lb 2 oz) chicken
40 g (1½ oz) butter, melted
1 tablespoon oil
1 tablespoon soy sauce
1 garlic clove, crushed
375 ml (13 fl oz/1½ cups) chicken stock
1 tablespoon plain (all-purpose) flour

serves 6

method Preheat the oven to 180°C (350°F/Gas 4). Cook the bacon in a dry frying pan over high heat for 5 minutes, or until crisp. Cut the bread into 1 cm (½ inch) cubes and place in a bowl. Mix in the bacon, spring onion, pecans, currants, parsley and combined egg and milk. Season with salt and freshly ground pepper.

Remove the giblets and any large amounts of fat from the cavity of the chicken. Pat the chicken dry with paper towels. Spoon the bacon mixture into the chicken cavity. Tuck the wing tips under the chicken and tie the legs securely with string.

Place the chicken on a rack in a deep baking dish. Brush with the combined butter, oil and soy sauce. Pour any remaining mixture into the baking dish with the garlic and half the stock. Roast the chicken for 1–1¼ hours, or until brown and tender, basting occasionally with the pan juices. Pierce the thighs and check that any juices running out are clear. If they are pink, continue cooking. Cover the chicken loosely with foil and leave in a warm place for 5 minutes before carving.

Discard all but 1 tablespoon of the pan juices from the baking dish. Transfer the baking dish to the stove. Add the flour to the pan juices and blend to a smooth paste. Stir constantly over low heat for 5 minutes, or until the mixture browns. Gradually add the remaining stock and stir until the mixture boils and thickens. Add a little extra stock or water if needed. Season and strain into a jug. Serve the chicken with the sauce.

family chicken pie

pastry

250 g (9 oz/2 cups) self-raising flour
125 g (5 oz) butter, chopped
1 egg

filling

1 barbecued chicken
30 g (1 oz) butter
1 onion, finely chopped
310 g (11 oz) tinned creamed corn
310 ml (11 fl oz/1¼ cups) cream

serves 6

method To make the pastry, process the flour and butter in a food processor for 15 seconds, until the mixture is fine and crumbly. Add the egg and 2–3 tablespoons water and process for 30 seconds, or until the mixture just comes together. Turn onto a lightly floured surface and gather together into a smooth ball. Cover with plastic wrap and refrigerate for 20 minutes.

Meanwhile, to make the filling, remove the meat from the chicken carcass and shred finely. Heat the butter in a frying pan and cook the onion over medium heat for 3 minutes. Add the chicken, creamed corn and cream. Bring to the boil, then reduce the heat and simmer for 10 minutes. Remove from the heat and allow to cool slightly.

Preheat the oven to 180°C (350°F/Gas 4). Roll half the pastry between two sheets of plastic wrap to cover the base and side of a 23 cm (9 inch) pie dish. Spoon the chicken mixture into the pastry shell.

Roll the remaining pastry to cover the top of the pie. Brush with milk. Press the edges together to seal. Trim the edges with a sharp knife. Roll the excess pastry into two long ropes and twist together. Brush the pie edge with a little milk and place the pastry rope around the rim. Bake the pie for 45 minutes, or until pastry is golden.

chicken with redcurrant sauce

4 chicken leg quarters (marylands)
125 ml (4 fl oz/½ cup) red wine
1 tablespoon finely chopped thyme
1 tablespoon finely chopped rosemary,
   plus extra, to serve
1 tablespoon olive oil
160 g (6 oz/½ cup) redcurrant jelly

serves 4

method Trim the chicken of excess fat and sinew. Place the chicken in a shallow non-metallic dish. Combine the wine, thyme and rosemary in a small bowl and pour over the chicken. Refrigerate, covered, for 2 hours or overnight, turning the chicken occasionally.

Preheat the oven to 200°C (400°F/Gas 6). Drain the chicken, reserving the marinade. Put the chicken in a baking dish and brush with the oil. Bake for 30 minutes, until cooked through, turning occasionally.

Meanwhile, combine the reserved marinade and redcurrant jelly in a small saucepan. Stir over medium heat until smooth, then bring to the boil. Reduce the heat and simmer, uncovered, for 15 minutes. Pour the sauce over the chicken and sprinkle with rosemary.

roast garlic chicken with vegetables

310 g (11 oz) orange sweet potatoes,
peeled and cut into wedges
310 g (11 oz) pontiac potatoes,
peeled and cut into wedges
310 g (11 oz) pumpkin (winter squash),
peeled and cut into wedges
1 chicken, cut into 8 pieces, or 1.5 kg
(3 lb 5 oz) chicken pieces
60 ml (2 fl oz/¼ cup) olive oil
1 tablespoon thyme
20 large garlic cloves, unpeeled (see Note)
½ teaspoon sea salt

serves 4

method Preheat the oven to 220°C (425°F/Gas 7). Put the chicken and vegetables in a baking dish, drizzle with the olive oil and scatter with the thyme leaves and garlic cloves. Sprinkle with the sea salt.

Roast for 1 hour 15 minutes, turning every 20 minutes, or until the chicken, sweet potato, potato and pumpkin are well browned and crisp at the edges. Serve immediately.

note *This may seem a lot of garlic, but it loses its pungency when roasted, becoming sweet and mild. To eat the garlic, squeeze the creamy roasted flesh from the skins and over the chicken and vegetables.*

A

agnolotti with chicken and buttered
   sage sauce 55
apricot chicken 109
Asian chicken and noodle soup 9

B

barbecued garlic chicken 84
beans, spicy chicken and 101
biryani 60
bolognaise, spaghetti with chicken 51
buffalo wings with ranch dressing 80
burger, chicken, with tangy garlic
   mayonnaise 78

C

Caesar salad, smoked chicken 34
cannelloni, chicken and pumpkin 47
capsicum, roasted capsicum and
   smoked chicken soup 10
chargrilled chicken 82
cheese
   chicken and bacon gougère 117
   conchiglie with chicken and
     ricotta 49
Chiang Mai noodles 75
chicken liver
   pâté with pistachio nuts 21
   tagliatelle with chicken livers and
     cream 52
chickpeas, braised chicken with 95
chilli garlic dip 86
chow mein 59
citrus
   chicken and citrus salad with curry
     dressing 31
   chicken and lime curry 93
   citrus chicken drumsticks 89
see also lemon
cobbler, chicken and leek 114
coconut and chicken soup 11
conchiglie with chicken and ricotta 49
coq au vin 102
creamy chicken, sage and tarragon
    pie 112
creamy chicken with mushrooms 106
creamy tomato and chicken stew 104
cucumber and yoghurt dressing 32
curry
   chicken and citrus salad with curry
     dressing 31
   chicken curry bags 19
   chicken curry laksa 14
   chicken curry puffs 26
   chicken and lime curry 93
   chicken and peanut panang
     curry 96
   chicken and spinach curry 105
   curried rice noodles with
     chicken 69
   green chicken curry 108
   red curry chicken salad 38
   Vietnamese chicken curry 103

D

donburi 74

E

eggplant, baked, with chicken and
   tomato 115

F

fajitas, chicken 88
family chicken pie 123
fettuccine with chicken and
   mushroom sauce 45
fruit medley, chicken breast
   with 83

G

garlic
   barbecued garlic chicken 84
   chicken burger with tangy garlic
     mayonnaise 78
   roast garlic chicken with
     vegetables 125
   spicy garlic chicken 99
   Thai chicken cutlets 86
Goan-style chicken with almonds 70
gougère, chicken and bacon 117
green chicken curry 108

H

herbs
   chicken agnolotti with buttered sage
     sauce 55
   chicken pot pies with herb
     scones 118
   herbed chicken soup 8
honey
   honey chicken 71
   honey-glazed chicken
     breasts 79
   spring chicken with honey
     glaze 113

I

Italian-style chicken pasta
   salad 39

L

laksa, chicken curry 14
lasagne, chicken and vegetable 53
leeks
   chicken and leek cobbler 114
   chicken and leek parcels 25
lemon
   chicken and lemon meatballs 18
   lemon chicken 58
   lemongrass chicken skewers 24

M

meatballs
   chicken and lemon 18
   spaghetti with chicken 46
mole 98
Moroccan chicken filo pie 119
mulligatawny 12

mushrooms
   chicken and mushroom casserole 97
   creamy chicken with mushrooms 106
   fettuccine with chicken and mushroom
     sauce 45
mustard chicken and asparagus
   quiche 121

N

nasi goreng 73
noodles
   Asian chicken and noodle soup 9
   Chiang Mai noodles 75
   chicken noodle soup 15
   curried rice noodles with
     chicken 69
   fried crispy noodles 67

O

olives and sun-dried tomatoes, chicken
   with 72
one-pots
   apricot chicken 109
   braised chicken with chickpeas 95
   chicken cacciatore 92
   chicken and lime curry 93
   chicken mole 98
   chicken and mushroom casserole 97
   chicken and orange casserole 100
   chicken paprika 107
   chicken and peanut panang
     curry 96
   chicken and spinach curry 105
   coq au vin 102
   creamy chicken with mushrooms 106
   creamy tomato and chicken
     stew 104
   Persian chicken 94
   spicy chicken and beans 101
   spicy garlic chicken 99
   Vietnamese chicken curry 103

P

Pacific chicken salad 37
pan-fries
   chicken biryani 60
   chicken donburi 74
   chicken pilaf with spices 68
   chicken with vegetables 61
   rice with chicken and seafood 64
   stuffed chicken breast 65
papaya, Vietnamese papaya and
   chicken salad 36
paprika chicken 107
parcels
   chicken and leek 25
   chicken and sugar snap pea 116
pasta
   chicken agnolotti with buttered sage
     sauce 55
   chicken and pumpkin cannelloni 47
   chicken ravioli 44
   chicken ravioli with fresh tomato
     sauce 50

chicken tortellini with tomato
sauce 48
chicken and vegetable lasagne 53
conchiglie with chicken and
ricotta 49
fettuccine with chicken and mushroom
sauce 45
Italian-style chicken pasta salad 39
spaghetti with chicken
bolognaise 51
spaghetti with chicken meatballs 46
spicy chicken broth with coriander
pasta 13
stir-fried chicken and pasta 54
succulent chicken and pasta salad 33
tagliatelle with chicken livers and
cream 52
pâté, chicken liver, with pistachio
nuts 21

peas
chicken and snow pea salad 30
chicken and sugar snap pea
parcels 116
Persian chicken 94

pies
chicken and bacon gougère 117
chicken pot pies with herb
scones 118
creamy chicken, sage and
tarragon 112
family chicken pie 123
Moroccan chicken filo pie 119
pot pies, chicken, with herb
scones 118

pumpkin
chicken and pumpkin cannelloni 47
pumpkin and pesto chicken in filo
pastry 23

Q
quesadillas 22
quiche, mustard chicken and asparagus 121

R
ranch dressing 80

ravioli
chicken ravioli 44
chicken ravioli with fresh tomato
sauce 50
red curry chicken salad 38
redcurrant sauce, chicken with 124

rice
chicken donburi 74
chicken pilaf with spices 68
mulligatawny 12
nasi goreng 73
rice with chicken and seafood 64

roasts
roast chicken with breadcrumb
stuffing 122
roast garlic chicken with
vegetables 125
spring chicken with honey glaze 113

S
salads
chicken and citrus salad with
curry dressing 31
chicken and snow pea 30
chicken and watercress 41
Italian-style chicken pasta 39
Pacific chicken salad 37
red curry chicken 38
smoked chicken Caesar salad 34
succulent chicken and pasta
salad 33
tandoori chicken salad 32
Thai chicken 35
Vietnamese papaya and chicken
salad 36
warm chicken salad 40
satay, chicken, with peanut sauce 20

seafood
nasi goreng 73
rice with chicken and seafood 64
Sichuan pepper chicken stir-fry 62

skewers
chicken satay with peanut
sauce 20
chicken tikka 27
lemongrass chicken 24
smoked chicken breast 85

soup
Asian chicken and noodle
soup 9
chicken and coconut 11
chicken curry laksa 14
chicken noodle soup 15
chicken and vegetable soup 17
creamy spinach and chicken 16
herbed chicken soup 8
mulligatawny 12
roasted capsicum and smoked
chicken 10
spicy chicken broth with coriander
pasta 13
tom kha gai 11
spaghetti with chicken bolognaise 51
spaghetti with chicken meatballs 46
spicy chicken and beans 101
spicy chicken broth with coriander
pasta 13
spicy garlic chicken 99
spicy spatchcocked chicken 120

spinach
chicken and spinach curry 105
creamy spinach and chicken
soup 16
pumpkin and pesto chicken in
filo pastry 23
spring chicken with honey
glaze 113

starters
chicken curry bags 19
chicken curry puffs 26
chicken and leek parcels 25
chicken and lemon meatballs 18

chicken liver pâté with pistachio
nuts 21
chicken quesadillas 22
chicken satay with peanut sauce 20
chicken tikka 27
lemongrass chicken skewers 24
pumpkin and pesto chicken in filo
pastry 23
see also soup

stir-fries
Chiang Mai noodles 75
chicken and cashew 63
chicken chow mein 59
chicken with olives and sun-dried
tomatoes 72
chicken with oyster sauce and basil 66
chicken and pasta 54
curried rice noodles with chicken 69
fried crispy noodles 67
Goan-style chicken with almonds 70
honey chicken 71
lemon chicken 58
nasi goreng 73
Sichuan pepper chicken 62

T
tagliatelle with chicken livers and
cream 52
tandoori barbecue chicken 81
tandoori chicken salad 32
teriyaki chicken wings 87
Thai chicken cutlets 86
Thai chicken salad 35
tom kha gai 11

tomato
chicken with baked eggplant and
tomato 115
chicken cacciatore 92
chicken mole 98
chicken with olives and sun-dried
tomatoes 72
chicken ravioli with fresh tomato
sauce 50
chicken tortellini with tomato
sauce 48
creamy tomato and chicken stew 104
stir-fried chicken and pasta 54
tortellini, chicken, with tomato
sauce 48

V
vegetables
chicken and vegetable lasagne 53
chicken and vegetable soup 17
pan-fried chicken with vegetables 61
roast garlic chicken with vegetables 125
see also leeks; pumpkin; salads; spinach
Vietnamese chicken curry 103
Vietnamese papaya and chicken
salad 36

W
warm chicken salad 40
watercress and chicken salad 41

Published in 2010 by Bay Books,
an imprint of Murdoch Books Pty Limited.

Murdoch Books Australia
Pier 8/9,
23 Hickson Road,
Millers Point NSW 2000
Phone: +61 (0)2 8220 2000
Fax: +61 (0)2 8220 2558
www.murdochbooks.com.au

Murdoch Books UK Limited
Erico House,
6th Floor North, 93–99 Upper Richmond Road,
Putney, London SW15 2TG
Phone: + 44 (0) 20 8785 5995
Fax: + 44 (0) 20 8785 5985
www.murdochbooks.co.uk

Chief Executive: Juliet Rogers

Publisher: Lynn Lewis
Senior Designer: Heather Menzies
Designer: Katy Wall
Editor: Justine Harding
Editorial Coordinator: Liz Malcolm
Index: Jo Rudd
Production: Alexandra Gonzalez

National Library of Australia Cataloguing-in-Publication Data:
Title: Chicken.
ISBN: 978-1-74266-000-4 (pbk.)
Series: 100 easy recipes
Notes: Includes index.
Subjects: Cooking (Chicken)
641.665

Printed by C & C Offset Printing Co. Ltd. PRINTED IN CHINA.

©Text, design and photography Murdoch Books Pty Limited 2010.